The Botanic Garden. Part II. Containing The Loves of the Plants. A Poem. With Philosophical Notes.

by

Erasmus Darwin

The Echo Library 2007

Published by

The Echo Library

Echo Library
131 High St.
Teddington
Middlesex TW11 8HH

www.echo-library.com

Please report serious faults in the text to complaints@echo-library.com

ISBN 978-1-40681-833-8

VIVUNT IN VENEREM FRONDES; NEMUS OMNE PER ALTUM
FELIX ARBOR AMAT; NUTANT AD MUTUA PALMÆ
FÆDERA, POPULEO SUSPIRAT POPULUS ICTU,
ET PLATANI PLATANIS, ALNOQUE ASSIBILAT ALNUS.

CLAUD. EPITH.

PREFACE.

Linneus has divided the vegetable world into 24 Classes; these Classes into about 120 Orders; these Orders contain about 2000 Families, or Genera; and these Families about 20,000 Species; besides the innumerable Varieties, which the accidents of climate or cultivation have added to these Species.

The Classes are distinguished from each other in this ingenious system, by the number, situation, adhesion, or reciprocal proportion of the males in each flower. The Orders, in many of these Classes, are distinguished by the number, or other circumstances of the females. The Families, or Genera, are characterized by the analogy of all the parts of the flower or fructification. The Species are distinguished by the foliage of the plant; and the Varieties by any accidental circumstance of colour, taste, or odour; the seeds of these do not always produce plants similar to the parent; as in our numerous fruit-trees and garden flowers; which are propagated by grafts or layers.

The first eleven Classes include the plants, in whose flowers both the sexes reside; and in which the Males or Stamens are neither united, nor unequal in height when at maturity; and are therefore distinguished from each other simply by the number of males in each flower, as is seen in the annexed PLATE, copied from the Dictionaire Botanique of M. BULLIARD, in which the numbers of each division refer to the Botanic Classes.

CLASS I. ONE MALE, *Monandria*; includes the plants which possess but One Stamen in each flower.

II. TWO MALES, *Diandria.* Two Stamens.

III. THREE MALES, *Triandria.* Three Stamens.

IV. FOUR MALES, *Tetrandria.* Four Stamens.

V. FIVE MALES, *Pentandria.* Five Stamens.

VI. SIX MALES, *Hexandria.* Six Stamens.

VII. SEVEN MALES, *Heptandria.* Seven Stamens.

VIII. EIGHT MALES, *Octandria.* Eight Stamens.

IX. NINE MALES, *Enneandria.* Nine Stamens.

X. TEN MALES, *Decandria.* Ten Stamens.

XI. TWELVE MALES, *Dodecandria.* Twelve Stamens.

The next two Classes are distinguished not only by the number of equal and disunited males, as in the above eleven Classes, but require an additional circumstance to be attended to, *viz.* whether the males or stamens be situated on the calyx, or not.

XII. TWENTY MALES, *Icosandria.* Twenty Stamens inserted on the calyx or flower-cup; as is well seen in the last Figure of No. xii. in the annexed Plate.

XIII. MANY MALES, *Polyandria*. From 20 to 100 Stamens, which do not adhere to the calyx; as is well seen in the first Figure of No. xiii. in the annexed Plate.

In the next two Classes, not only the number of stamens are to be observed, but the reciprocal proportions in respect to height.

XIV. TWO POWERS, *Didynamia*. Four Stamens, of which two are lower than the other two; as is seen in the two first Figures of No. xiv.

XV. FOUR POWERS, *Tetradynamia*. Six Stamens; of which four are taller, and the two lower ones opposite to each other; as is seen in the third Figure of the upper row in No. 15.

The five subsequent Classes are distinguished not by the number of the males, or stamens, but by their union or adhesion, either by their anthers, or filaments, or to the female or pistil.

XVI. ONE BROTHERHOOD, *Monadelphia*. Many Stamens united by their filaments into one company; as in the second Figure below of No. xvi.

XVII. TWO BROTHERHOODS, *Diadelphia*. Many Stamens united by their filaments into two Companies; as in the uppermost Fig. No. xvii.

XVIII. MANY BROTHERHOODS, *Polyadelphia*. Many Stamens united by their filaments into three or more companies, as in No. xviii.

XIX. CONFEDERATE MALES, *Syngenesia*. Many Stamens united by their anthers; as in first and second Figures, No. xix.

XX. FEMININE MALES, *Gynandria*. Many Stamens attached to the pistil.

The next three Classes consist of plants, whose flowers contain but one of the sexes; or if some of them contain both sexes, there are other flowers accompanying them of but one sex.

XXI. ONE HOUSE, *Monoecia*. Male flowers and female flowers separate, but on the same plant.

XXII. TWO HOUSES, *Dioecia*. Male flowers and female flowers separate, on different plants.

XXIII. POLYGAMY, *Polygamia*. Male and female flowers on one or more plants, which have at the same time flowers of both sexes.

The last Class contains the plants whose flowers are not discernible.

XXIV. CLANDESTINE MARRIAGE, *Cryptogamia*.

The Orders of the first thirteen Classes are founded on the number of Females, or Pistils, and distinguished by the names, ONE FEMALE, *Monogynia*. TWO FEMALES, *Digynia*. THREE FEMALES, *Trigynia*, &c. as is seen in No. i.

which represents a plant of one male, one female; and in the first Figure of No. xi. which represents a flower with twelve males, and three females; (for, where the pistils have no apparent styles, the summits, or stigmas, are to be numbered) and in the first Figure of No. xii. which represents a flower with twenty males and many females; and in the last Figure of the same No. which has twenty males and one female; and in No. xiii. which represents a flower with many males and many females.

The Class of TWO POWERS, is divided into two natural Orders; into such as have their seeds naked at the bottom of the calyx, or flower cup; and such as have their seeds covered; as is seen in No. xiv. Fig. 3. and 5.

The Class of FOUR POWERS, is divided also into two Orders; in one of these the seeds are inclosed in a silicule, as in *Shepherd's purse*. No. xiv. Fig. 5. In the other they are inclosed in a silique, as in *Wall-flower*. Fig. 4.

In all the other Classes, excepting the Classes Confederate Males, and Clandestine Marriage, as the character of each Class is distinguished by the situations of the males; the character of the Orders is marked by the numbers of them. In the Class ONE BROTHERHOOD, No. xvi. Fig. 3. the Order of ten males is represented. And in the Class TWO BROTHERHOODS, No. xvii. Fig. 2. the Order ten males is represented.

In the Class CONFEDERATE MALES, the Orders are chiefly distinguished by the fertility or barrenness of the florets of the disk, or ray of the compound flower.

And in the Class of CLANDESTINE MARRIAGE, the four Orders are termed FERNS, MOSSES, FLAGS, and FUNGUSSES.

The Orders are again divided into Genera, or Families, which are all natural associations, and are described from the general resemblances of the parts of fructification, in respect to their number, form, situation, and reciprocal proportion. These are the Calyx, or Flower-cup, as seen in No. iv. Fig. 1. No. x. Fig. 1. and 3. No. xiv. Fig. 1. 2. 3. 4. Second, the Corol, or Blossom, as seen in No. i. ii. &c. Third, the Males, or Stamens; as in No. iv. Fig. 1. and No. viii. Fig. 1. Fourth, the Females, or Pistils; as in No. i. No. xii. Fig. 1. No. xiv. Fig. 3. No. xv. Fig. 3. Fifth, the Pericarp or Fruit-vessel; as No. xv. Fig. 4. 5. No. xvii. Fig. 2. Sixth, the Seeds.

The illustrious author of the Sexual System of Botany, in his preface to his account of the Natural Orders, ingeniously imagines, that one plant of each Natural Order was created in the beginning; and that the intermarriages of these produced one plant of every Genus, or Family; and that the intermarriages of these Generic, or Family plants, produced all the Species: and lastly, that the intermarriages of the individuals of the Species produced the Varieties.

In the following POEM, the name or number of the Class or Order of each plant is printed in italics; as "*Two* brother swains." "*One* House contains them." and the word "*secret*" expresses the Class of Clandestine Marriage.

The Reader, who wishes to become further acquainted with this delightful field of science, is advised to study the words of the Great Master, and is apprized that they are exactly and literally translated into English, by a Society at LICHFIELD, in four Volumes Octavo.

To the SYSTEM OF VEGETABLES is prefixed a copious explanation of all the Terms used in Botany, translated from a thesis of Dr. ELMSGREEN, with the plates and references from the Philosophia Botannica of LINNEUS.

To the FAMILIES OF PLANTS is prefixed a Catalogue of the names of plants, and other Botanic Terms, carefully accented, to shew their proper pronunciation; a work of great labour, and which was much wanted, not only by beginners, but by proficients in BOTANY.

— describing the theory of evolution

8

PROEM. : *prologue to a poem*

GENTLE READER!

Lo, here a CAMERA OBSCURA is presented to thy view, in which are lights and shades dancing on a whited canvas, and magnified into apparent life!—if thou art perfectly at leasure for such trivial amusement, walk in, and view the wonders of my INCHANTED GARDEN. *magie*

Whereas P. OVIDIUS NASO, a great Necromancer in the famous Court of AUGUSTUS CAESAR, did by art poetic transmute Men, Women, and even Gods and Goddesses, into Trees and Flowers; I have undertaken by similar art to restore some of them to their original animality, after having remained prisoners so long in their respective vegetable mansions; and have here exhibited them before thee. Which thou may'st contemplate as diverse little pictures suspended over the chimney of a Lady's dressing-room, *connected only by a slight festoon of ribbons*. And which, though thou may'st not be acquainted with the originals, may amuse thee by the beauty of their persons, their graceful attitudes, or the brilliancy of their dress.

FAREWELL.

*[handwritten: * illustrates Linnaeus's Classification scheme]*

THE LOVES OF THE PLANTS.

CANTO I.

[handwritten left margin: view descends microscopic/Human view]

[handwritten: slender graceful woman] *[handwritten: gathering]*

Descend, ye hovering Sylphs! aerial Quires,
And sweep with little hands your silver lyres;
With fairy footsteps print your grassy rings,
Ye Gnomes! accordant to the tinkling strings;
5   While in soft notes I tune to oaten reed   *[handwritten: alcohol]*
Gay hopes, and amorous sorrows of the mead.—
From giant Oaks, that wave their branches dark,
To the dwarf Moss, that clings upon their bark,
What Beaux and Beauties crowd the gaudy groves,
10 And woo and win their vegetable Loves.
How Snowdrops cold, and blue-eyed Harebels blend
Their tender tears, as o'er the stream they bend;
The lovesick Violet, and the Primrose pale
Bow their sweet heads, and whisper to the gale;
15 With secret sighs the Virgin Lily droops,
And jealous Cowslips hang their tawny cups.
How the young Rose in beauty's damask pride
Drinks the warm blushes of his bashful bride;
With honey'd lips enamour'd Woodbines meet,
20 Clasp with fond arms, and mix their kisses sweet.—

Stay thy soft-murmuring waters, gentle Rill;
Hush, whispering Winds, ye rustling Leaves, be still;
Rest, silver Butterflies, your quivering wings;
Alight, ye Beetles, from your airy rings;

[*Vegetable Loves.* l. 10. Linneus, the celebrated Swedish naturalist, has demonstrated, that all flowers contain families of males or females, or both; and on their marriages has constructed his invaluable system of Botany.]

25 Ye painted Moths, your gold-eyed plumage furl,
Bow your wide horns, your spiral trunks uncurl;
Glitter, ye Glow-worms, on your mossy beds;
Descend, ye Spiders, on your lengthen'd threads;
Slide here, ye horned Snails, with varnish'd shells;
30 Ye Bee-nymphs, listen in your waxen cells!—

BOTANIC MUSE! who in this latter age
Led by your airy hand the Swedish sage,
Bad his keen eye your secret haunts explore
On dewy dell, high wood, and winding shore;

35   Say on each leaf how tiny Graces dwell;
    How laugh the Pleasures in a blossom's bell;
    How insect Loves arise on cobweb wings,
    Aim their light shafts, and point their little stings.

    First the tall CANNA lifts his curled brow
40   Erect to heaven, and plights his nuptial vow;

or relating to marriage

[*Canna.* l. 39. Cane, or Indian Reed. One male and one female inhabit each flower. It is brought from between the tropics to our hot-houses, and bears a beautiful crimson flower; the seeds are used as shot by the Indians, and are strung for prayer-beads in some catholic countries.]

    The virtuous pair, in milder regions born,
    Dread the rude blast of Autumn's icy morn;
    Round the chill fair he folds his crimson vest,
    And clasps the timorous beauty to his breast.

45   Thy love, CALLITRICHE, *two* Virgins share,
    Smit with thy starry eye and radiant hair;—
    On the green margin sits the youth, and laves
    His floating train of tresses in the waves;
    Sees his fair features paint the streams that pass,
50   And bends for ever o'er the watery glass.

    Two brother swains, of COLLIN'S gentle name,
    The same their features, and their forms the same,

[*Callitriche*, l. 45. Fine-Hair, Stargrass. One male and two females inhabit each flower. The upper leaves grow in form of a star, whence it is called Stellaria Aquatica by Ray and others; its stems and leaves float far on the water, and are often so matted together, as to bear a person walking on them. The male sometimes lives in a separate flower.]

[*Collinsonia.* l. 51. Two males one female. I have lately observed a very singular circumstance in this flower; the two males stand widely diverging from each other, and the female bends herself into contact first with one of them, and after some time leaves this, and applies herself to the other. It is probable one of the anthers may be mature before the other? See note on Gloriosa, and Genista. The females in Nigella, devil in the bush, are very tall compared to the males; and bending over in a circle to them, give the flower some resemblance to a regal crown. The female of the epilobium angustisolium, rose bay willow herb, bends down amongst the males for several days, and becomes upright again when impregnated.]

[*Genista.* l. 57. Dyer's broom. Ten males and one female inhabit this flower. The males are generally united at the bottom in two sets, whence Linneus has named the class "two brotherhoods." In the Genista, however, they are united in but one set. The flowers of this class are called papilionaceous, from their resemblance to a butterfly, as the pea-blossom. In the Spartium Scoparium, or common broom, I have lately observed a curious circumstance, the males or stamens are in two sets, one set rising a quarter of an inch above the other; the upper set does not arrive at their maturity so soon as the lower, and the stigma, or head of the female, is produced amongst the upper or immature set; but as soon as the pistil grows tall enough to burst open the keel-leaf, or hood of the flower, it bends itself round in an instant, like a French horn, and inserts its head, or stigma, amongst the lower or mature set of males. The pistil, or female, continues to grow in length; and in a few days the stigma arrives again amongst the upper set, by the time they become mature. This wonderful contrivance is readily seen by opening the keel-leaf of the flowers of broom before they burst spontaneously. See note on Collinsonia, Gloriosa, Draba.]

> With rival love for fair COLLINIA sigh,
> Knit the dark brow, and roll the unsteady eye.
> 55   With sweet concern the pitying beauty mourns,
> And sooths with smiles the jealous pair by turns.
>
> Sweet blooms GENISTA in the myrtle shade,
> And *ten* fond brothers woo the haughty maid.
> *Two* knights before thy fragrant altar bend,
> 60   Adored MELISSA! and *two* squires attend.
> MEADIA'S soft chains *five* suppliant beaux confess,
> And hand in hand the laughing belle address;
> Alike to all, she bows with wanton air,
> Rolls her dark eye, and waves her golden hair.

[*Melissa.* l. 60. Balm. In each flower there are four males and one female; two of the males stand higher than the other two; whence the name of the class "two powers." I have observed in the Ballota, and others of this class, that the two lower stamens, or males become mature before the two higher. After they have shed their dust, they turn themselves away outwards; and the pistil, or female, continuing to grow a little taller, is applied to the upper stamens. See Gloriosa, and Genista.

All the plants of this class, which have naked seeds, are aromatic. The Marum, and Nepeta are particularly delightful to cats; no other brute animals seem pleased with any odours but those of their food or prey.]

[*Meadia.* l. 61. Dodecatheon, American Cowslip. Five males and one female. The males, or anthers, touch each other. The uncommon beauty of this flower occasioned Linneus to give it a name signifying the twelve heathen gods; and Dr. Mead to affix his own name to it. The pistil is much longer than the stamens, hence the flower-stalks have their elegant bend, that the stigma may hang downwards to receive the fecundating dust of the anthers. And the petals are so beautifully turned back to prevent the rain or dew drops from sliding down and washing off this dust prematurely; and at the same time exposing it to the light and air. As soon as the seeds are formed, it erects all the flower-stalks to prevent them from falling out; and thus loses the beauty of its figure. Is this a mechanical effect, or does it indicate a vegetable storgé to preserve its offspring? See note on Ilex, and Gloriosa.

In the Meadia, the Borago, Cyclamen, Solanum, and many others, the filaments are very short compared with the slyle. Hence it became necessary, 1st. to furnish the stamens with long anthers. 2d. To lengthen and bend the peduncle or flower-slalk, that the flower might hang downwards. 3d. To reflect the petals. 4th. To erect these peduncles when the germ was fecundated. We may reason upon this by observing, that all this apparatus might have been spared, if the filaments alone had grown longer; and that thence in these flowers that the filaments are the most unchangeable parts; and that thence their comparative length, in respect to the style, would afford a most permanent mark of their generic character.]

> 65 Woo'd with long care, CURCUMA cold and shy
>   Meets her fond husband with averted eye:
>   *Four* beardless youths the obdurate beauty move
>   With soft attentions of Platonic love.
>
>   With vain desires the pensive ALCEA burns,
> 70   And, like sad ELOISA, loves and mourns.
>   The freckled IRIS owns a fiercer flame,
>   And *three* unjealous husbands wed the dame.
>   CUPRESSUS dark disdains his dusky bride,
>   *One* dome contains them, but *two* beds divide.
> 75   The proud OSYRIS flies his angry fair,
>   *Two* houses hold the fashionable pair.

[*Curcuma.* l. 65. Turmeric. One male and one female inhabit this flower; but there are besides four imperfect males, or filaments without anthers upon them, called by Linneus eunuchs. The flax of our country has ten filaments, and but five of them are terminated with anthers; the Portugal flax has ten perfect males, or stamens; the Verbena of our country has four males; that of Sweden has but two; the genus Albuca, the Bignonia Catalpa, Gratiola, and hemlock-leaved Geranium have only half their filaments crowned with anthers. In like manner the florets, which form the rays of the flowers of the order frustraneous polygamy of the class syngenesia, or confederate males, as the sun-flower, are furnished with a style only, and no stigma: and are thence barren. There is also a style without a stigma in the whole order dioecia gynandria; the male flowers of which are thence barren. The Opulus is another plant, which contains some unprolific flowers. In like manner some tribes of insects have males, females, and neuters among them: as bees, wasps, ants.

There is a curious circumstance belonging to the class of insects which have two wings, or diptera, analogous to the rudiments of stamens above described; viz. two little knobs are found placed each on a stalk or peduncle, generally under a little arched scale; which appear to be rudiments of hinder wings; and are called by Linneus, halteres, or poisers, a term of his introduction. A.T. Bladh. Amaen. Acad. V. 7. Other animals have marks of having in a long process of time undergone changes in some parts of their bodies, which may have been effected to accommodate them to new ways of procuring their food. The existence of teats on the breasts of male animals, and which are generally replete with a thin kind of milk at their nativity, is a wonderful instance of this kind. Perhaps all the productions of nature are in their progress to greater perfection? an idea countenanced by the modern discoveries and deductions concerning the progressive formation of the solid parts of the terraqueous globe, and consonant to the dignity of the Creator of all things.]

[*Alcea*, l. 69. Flore pleno. Double hollyhock. The double flowers, so much admired by the florists, are termed by the botanist vegetable monsters; in some of these the petals are multiplied three or four times, but without excluding the stamens, hence they produce some seeds, as Campanula and Stramoneum; but in others the petals become so numerous as totally to exclude the stamens, or males; as Caltha, Peonia, and Alcea; these produce no seeds, and are termed eunuchs. Philos. Botan. No. 150.

These vegetable monsters are formed in many ways. 1st. By the multiplication of the petals and the exclusion of the nectaries, as in larkspur. 2d. By the multiplication of the nectaries and exclusion of the petals; as in columbine. 3d. In some flowers growing in cymes, the wheel-shape flowers in the margin are multiplied to the exclusion of the bell-shape flowers in the centre; as in gelder-rose. 4th. By the elongation of the florets in the centre. Instances of both these are found in daisy and feverfew; for other kinds of vegetable monsters, see Plantago.

The perianth is not changed in double flowers, hence the genus or family may be often discovered by the calyx, as in Hepatica, Ranunculus, Alcea. In those flowers, which have many petals, the lowest series of the petals remains unchanged in respect to number; hence the natural number of the petals is easily discovered. As in poppies, roses, and Nigella, or devil in a bulb. Phil. Bot. p. 128.]

[*Iris*. l. 71. Flower de Luce. Three males, one female. Some of the species have a beautifully freckled flower; the large stigma or head of the female covers the three males, counterfeiting a petal with its divisions.]

[*Cupressus*. l. 73. Cypress. One House. The males live in separate flowers, but on the same plant. The males of some of these plants, which are in separate flowers from the females, have an elastic membrane; which disperses their dust to a considerable distance, when the anthers burst open. This dust, on a fine day, may often be seen like a cloud hanging round the common nettle. The males and females of all the cone-bearing plants are in separate flowers, either on the same or on different plants; they produce resins, and many of them are supposed to supply the most durable timber: what is called Venice-turpentine is obtained from the larch by wounding the bark about two feet from the ground, and catching it as it exsudes; Sandarach is procured from common juniper; and Incense from a juniper with yellow fruit. The unperishable chests, which contain the Egyptian mummies, were of Cypress; and the Cedar, with which black-lead pencils are covered, is not liable to be eaten by worms. See Miln's Bot. Dict. art. coniferæ. The gates of St. Peter's church at Rome, which had lasted from the time of Constantine to that of Pope Eugene the fourth, that is to say eleven hundred years, were of Cypress, and had in that time suffered no decay. According to Thucydides, the Athenians buried the bodies of their heroes in coffins of Cypress, as being not subject to decay. A similar durability has also been ascribed to Cedar. Thus Horace,

——speramus carmina fingi
Posse linenda cedre, & lavi servanda cupresso.

[*Osyris*. l. 75. Two houses. The males and females are on different plants. There are many instances on record, where female plants have been impregnated at very great distance from their male; the dust discharged from the anthers is very light, small, and copious, so that it may spread very wide in the atmosphere, and be carried to the distant pistils, without the supposition of any particular attraction; these plants resemble some insects, as the ants, and cochineal insect, of which the males have wings, but not the female.]

> With strange deformity PLANTAGO treads,
> A Monster-birth! and lifts his hundred heads;
> Yet with soft love a gentle belle he charms,
> 80   And clasps the beauty in his hundred arms.
> So hapless DESDEMONA, fair and young,
> Won by OTHELLO'S captivating tongue,
> Sigh'd o'er each strange and piteous tale, distress'd,
> And sunk enamour'd on his sooty breast.
>
> 85   *Two* gentle shepherds and their sister-wives
> With thee, ANTHOXA! lead ambrosial lives;

[*Plantago*. l. 77. Rosea. Rose Plantain. In this vegetable monster the bractes, or divisions of the spike, become wonderfully enlarged; and are converted into leaves. The chaffy scales of the calyx in Xeranthemum, and in a species of Dianthus, and the glume in some alpine grasses, and the scales of the ament in the salix rosea, rose willow, grow into leaves; and produce other kinds of monsters. The double flowers become monsters by the multiplication of their petals or nectaries. See note on Alcea.

[*Anthoxanthum*. l. 83. Vernal grass. Two males, two females. The other grasses have three males and two females. The flowers of this grass give the fragrant scent to hay. I am informed it is frequently viviparous, that is, that it bears sometimes roots or bulbs instead of seeds, which after a time drop off and strike root into the ground. This circumstance is said to obtain in many of the alpine grasses, whose seeds are perpetually devoured by small birds. The Festuca Dometorum, fescue grass of the bushes, produces bulbs from the sheaths of its straw. The Allium Magicum, or magical onion, produces onions on its head, instead of seeds. The Polygonum Viviparum, viviparous bistort, rises about a foot high, with a beautiful spike of flowers, which are succeeded by buds or bulbs, which fall off and take root. There is a bulb, frequently seen on birch-trees, like a bird's nest, which seems to be a similar attempt of nature, to produce another tree; which falling off might take root in spongy ground.

There is an instance of this double mode of production in the animal kingdom, which is equally extraordinary: the same species of Aphis is viviparous in summer, and oviparous in autumn. A. T. Bladh. Amoen. Acad. V. 7.]

> Where the wide heath in purple pride extends,
> And scatter'd furze its golden lustre blends,
> Closed in a green recess, unenvy'd lot!
> 90   The blue smoak rises from their turf-built cot;
> Bosom'd in fragrance blush their infant train,
> Eye the warm sun, or drink the silver rain.
>
> The fair OSMUNDA seeks the silent dell,
> The ivy canopy, and dripping cell;
> 95   There hid in shades *clandestine* rites approves,
> Till the green progeny betrays her loves.

[*Osmunda*. l. 93. This plant grows on moist rocks; the parts of its flower or its seeds are scarce discernible; whence Linneus has given the name of clandestine marriage to this class. The younger plants are of a beautiful vivid green.]

> With charms despotic fair CHONDRILLA reigns
> O'er the soft hearts of *five* fraternal swains;
> If sighs the changeful nymph, alike they mourn;
> 100 And, if she smiles, with rival raptures burn.
> So, tun'd in unison, Eolian Lyre!
> Sounds in sweet symphony thy kindred wire;
> Now, gently swept by Zephyr's vernal wings,
> Sink in soft cadences the love-sick strings;
> 105 And now with mingling chords, and voices higher,
> Peal the full anthems of the aerial choir.

[*Chondrilla*. l. 97. Of the class Confederate Males. The numerous florets, which constitute the disk of the flowers in this class, contain in each five males surrounding one female, which are connected at top, whence the name of the class. An Italian writer, in a discourse on the irritability of flowers, asserts, that if the top of the floret be touched, all the filaments which support the cylindrical anther will contrast themselves, and that by thus raising or depressing the anther the whole of the prolific dust is collected on the stigma. He adds, that if one filament be touched after it is separated from the floret, that it will contract like the muscular fibres of animal bodies, his experiments were tried on the Centauréa Calcitrapoides, and on artichokes, and globe-thistles. Discourse on the irratability of plants. Dodsley.]

Five sister-nymphs to join Diana's train
With thee, fair LYCHNIS! vow,—but vow in vain;
Beneath one roof resides the virgin band,
110 Flies the fond swain, and scorns his offer'd hand;
But when soft hours on breezy pinions move,
And smiling May attunes her lute to love,
Each wanton beauty, trick'd in all her grace,
Shakes the bright dew-drops from her blushing face;
115 In gay undress displays her rival charms,
And calls her wondering lovers to her arms.

When the young Hours amid her tangled hair
Wove the fresh rose-bud, and the lily fair,

[*Lychnis.* l. 108. Ten males and five females. The flowers which contain the five females, and those which contain the ten males, are found on different plants; and often at a great distance from each other. Five of the ten males arrive at their maturity some days before the other five, as may be seen by opening the corol before it naturally expands itself. When the females arrive at their maturity, they rise above the petals, as if looking abroad for their distant husbands; the scarlet ones contribute much to the beauty of our meadows in May and June.]

Proud GLORIOSA led *three* chosen swains,
120 The blushing captives of her virgin chains.—
—When Time's rude hand a bark of wrinkles spread
Round her weak limbs, and silver'd o'er her head,
Three other youths her riper years engage,
The flatter'd victims of her wily age.

125 So, in her wane of beauty, NINON won
With fatal smiles her gay unconscious son.—

[*Gloriosa.* l. 119. Superba. Six males, one female. The petals of this beautiful flower with three of the stamens, which are first mature, stand up in apparent disorder; and the pistil bends at nearly a right angle to insert its stigma amongst them. In a few days, as these decline, the other three stamens bend over, and approach the pistil. In the Fritillaria Persica, the six stamens are of equal lengths, and the anthers lie at a distance from the pistil, and three alternate ones approach first; and, when these decline, the other three approach: in the Lithrum Salicaria, (which has twelve males and one female) a beautiful red flower, which grows on the banks of rivers, six of the males arrive at maturity, and surround the female some time before the other six; when these decline, the other six rise up, and supply their places. Several other flowers have in similar manner two sets of stamens of different ages, as Adoxa, Lychnis, Saxifraga. See Genista. Perhaps a difference in the time of their maturity obtains in all these flowers, which have numerous stamens. In the Kahnia the ten stamens lie round the pistil like the radii of a wheel; and each anther is concealed in a nich of the corol to protect it from cold and moisture; these anthers rise separately from their niches, and approach the pistil for a time, and then recede to their former situations.]

> Clasp'd in his arms she own'd a mother's name,—
> "Desist, rash youth! restrain your impious flame,
> "First on that bed your infant-form was press'd,
> 130 "Born by my throes, and nurtured at my breast."—
> Back as from death he sprung, with wild amaze
> Fierce on the fair he fix'd his ardent gaze;
> Dropp'd on one knee, his frantic arms outspread,
> And stole a guilty glance toward the bed;
> 135 Then breath'd from quivering lips a whisper'd vow,
> And bent on heaven his pale repentant brow;
> "Thus, thus!" he cried, and plung'd the furious dart,
> And life and love gush'd mingled from his heart.
>
> The fell SILENE and her sisters fair,
> 140 Skill'd in destruction, spread the viscous snare.

[*Silene.* l. 139. Catchfly. Three females and ten males inhabit each flower; the viscous material, which surrounds the stalks under the flowers of this plant, and of the Cucubulus Otites, is a curious contrivance to prevent various insects from plundering the honey, or devouring the seed. In the Dionaea Muscipula there is a still more wonderful contrivance to prevent the depredations of insects: The leaves are armed with long teeth, like the antennæ of insects, and lie spread upon the ground round the stem; and are so irritable, that when an insect creeps upon them, they fold up, and crush or pierce it to death. The last professor Linneus, in his Supplementum Plantarum, gives the following account of the Arum Muscivorum. The flower has the smell of carrion; by which the flies are invited to lay their eggs in the chamber of the flower, but in vain endeavour to escape, being prevented by the hairs pointing inwards; and thus perish in the flower, whence its name of fly-eater. P. 411. in the Dypsacus is another contrivance for this purpose, a bason of water is placed round each joint of the stem. In the

Drosera is another kind of fly-trap. See Dypsacus and Drosera; the flowers of Siléne and Cucúbalus are closed all day, but are open and give an agreeable odour in the night. See Cerea. See additional notes at the end of the poem.]

> The harlot-band *ten* lofty bravoes screen,
> And frowning guard the magic nets unseen.—
> Haste, glittering nations, tenants of the air,
> Oh, steer from hence your viewless course afar!
> 145 If with soft words, sweet blushes, nods, and smiles,
> The *three* dread Syrens lure you to their toils,
> Limed by their art in vain you point your stings,
> In vain the efforts of your whirring wings!—
> Go, seek your gilded mates and infant hives,
> 150 Nor taste the honey purchas'd with your lives!

> When heaven's high vault condensing clouds deform,
> Fair AMARYLLIS flies the incumbent storm,

[*Amaryllis*, l. 152. Formosissima. Most beautiful Amaryllis. Six males, one female. Some of the bell-flowers close their apertures at night, or in rainy or cold weather, as the convolvulus, and thus protect their included stamens and pistils. Other bell-flowers hang their apertures downwards, as many of the lilies; in those the pistil, when at maturity, is longer than the stamens; and by this pendant attitude of the bell, when the anthers burst, their dust falls on the stigma: and these are at the same time sheltered as with an umbrella from rain and dews. But, as a free exposure to the air is necessary for their fecundation, the style and filaments in many of these flowers continue to grow longer after the bell is open, and hang down below its rim. In others, as in the martagon, the bell is deeply divided, and the divisions are reflected upwards, that they may not prevent the access of air, and at the same time afford some shelter from perpendicular rain or dew. Other bell-flowers, as the hemerocallis and amaryllis, have their bells nodding only, as it were, or hanging obliquely toward the horizon; which, as their stems are slender, turn like a weathercock from the wind; and thus very effectually preserve their inclosed stamens and anthers from the rain and cold. Many of these flowers, both before and after their season of fecundation, erect their heads perpendicular to the horizon, like the Meadia, which cannot be explained from meer mechanism.

The Amaryllis formosissima is a flower of the last mentioned kind, and affords an agreeable example of *art* in the vegetable economy, 1. The pistil is of great length compared with the stamens; and this I suppose to have been the most unchangeable part of the flower, as in Meadia, which see. 2. To counteract this circumstance, the pistil and stamens are made to decline downwards, that the prolific dust might fall from the anthers on the stigma. 3. To produce this effect, and to secure it when produced, the corol is lacerated, contrary to what occurs in other flowers of this genus, and the lowest division with the two next lowest ones are wrapped closely over the style and filaments, binding them forceibly down lower toward the horizon than the usual inclination of the bell in this genus, and thus constitutes a most elegant flower. There is another contrivance for this purpose in the Hemerocallis flava: the long pistil often is bent somewhat like the capital letter N, with design to shorten it, and thus to bring the stigma amongst the anthers.]

Seeks with unsteady step the shelter'd vale,
And turns her blushing beauties from the gale.—
155 *Six* rival youths, with soft concern impress'd,
Calm all her fears, and charm her cares to rest.—
So shines at eve the sun-illumin'd fane,
Lifts its bright cross, and waves its golden vane;
From every breeze the polish'd axle turns,
160 And high in air the dancing meteor burns.

Four of the giant brood with ILEX stand,
Each grasps a thousand arrows in his hand;

[*Ilex*. l. 161. Holly. Four males, four females. Many plants, like many animals, are furnished with arms for their protection; these are either aculei, prickles, as in rose and barberry, which are formed from the outer bark of the plant; or spinæ, thorns, as in hawthorn, which are an elongation of the wood, and hence more difficult to be torn off than the former; or stimuli, stings, as in the nettles, which are armed with a venomous fluid for the annoyance of naked animals. The shrubs and trees, which have prickles or thorns, are grateful food to many animals, as goosberry, and gorse; and would be quickly devoured, if not thus armed; the stings seem a protection against some kinds of insects, as well as the naked mouths of quadrupeds. Many plants lose their thorns by cultivation, as wild animals lose their ferocity; and some of them their horns. A curious circumstance attends the large hollies in Needwood-forest, they are armed with thorny leaves about eight feet high, and have smooth leaves above; as if they were conscious that horses and cattle could not reach their upper branches. See note on Meadia, and on Mancinella. The numerous clumps of hollies in Needwood-forest serve as landmarks to direct the travellers across it in various directions; and as a shelter to the deer and cattle in winter; and in scarce seasons supply them with much food. For when the upper branches, which are without prickles, are cut down, the deer crop the leaves and peel off the bark. The bird-lime made from the bark of hollies seems to be a very similar material to the elastic gum, or Indian rubber, as it is called. There is a fossile elastic bitumen found at Matlock in Derbyshire, which much resembles these substances in its elasticity and inflammability. The thorns of the mimosa cornigere resemble cow's horns in appearance as well as in use. System of Vegetables, p. 782.]

A thousand steely points on every scale

Form the bright terrors of his bristly male.—
165 So arm'd, immortal Moore uncharm'd the spell,
  And slew the wily dragon of the well.—
  Sudden with rage their *injur'd* bosoms burn,
  Retort the insult, or the wound return;
  Unwrong'd, as gentle as the breeze that sweeps
170 The unbending harvests or undimpled deeps,
  They guard, the Kings of Needwood's wide domains,
  Their sister-wives and fair infantine trains;
  Lead the lone pilgrim through the trackless glade,
  Or guide in leafy wilds the wand'ring maid.

175 So WRIGHT's bold pencil from Vesuvio's hight
  Hurls his red lavas to the troubled night;
  From Calpè starts the intolerable flash,
  Skies burst in flames, and blazing oceans dash;—
  Or bids in sweet repose his shades recede,
180 Winds the still vale, and slopes the velvet mead;
  On the pale stream expiring Zephyrs sink,
  And Moonlight sleeps upon its hoary brink.

  Gigantic Nymph! the fair KLEINHOVIA reigns,
  The grace and terror of Orixa's plains;

[*Hurls his red lavas.* l. 176. Alluding to the grand paintings of the eruptions of Vesuvius, and of the destruction of the Spanish vessels before Gibraltar; and to the beautiful landscapes and moonlight scenes, by Mr. Wright of Derby.]

[*Kleinhovia.* l. 183. In this class the males in each flower are supported by the female. The name of the class may be translated "Viragoes," or "Feminine Males."

The largest tree perhaps in the world is of the same natural order as Kleinhovia, it is the Adansonia, or Ethiopian Sour-gourd, or African Calabash tree. Mr. Adanson says the diameter of the trunk frequently exceeds 25 feet, and the horizontal branches are from 45 to 55 feet long, and so large that each branch is equal to the largest trees of Europe. The breadth of the top is from 120 to 150 feet. And one of the roots bared only in part by the wasting away of the earth by the river, near which it grew, measured 110 feet long; and yet these stupendous trees never exceed 70 feet in height. Voyage to Senegal.]

  O'er her warm cheek the blush of beauty swims,
  And nerves Herculean bend her sinewy limbs;
  With frolic eye she views the affrighted throng,
190 And shakes the meadows, as she towers along,
  With playful violence displays her charms,
  And bears her trembling lovers in her arms.

So fair THALESTRIS shook her plumy crest,
And bound in rigid mail her jutting breast;
195 Poised her long lance amid the walks of war,
And Beauty thunder'd from Bellona's car;
Greece arm'd in vain, her captive heroes wove
The chains of conquest with the wreaths of love.

When o'er the cultured lawns and dreary wastes
200 Retiring Autumn flings her howling blasts,
Bends in tumultuous waves the struggling woods,
And showers their leafy honours on the floods,
In withering heaps collects the flowery spoil,
And each chill insect sinks beneath the soil;
205 Quick flies fair TULIPA the loud alarms,
And folds her infant closer in her arms;
In some lone cave, secure pavilion, lies,
And waits the courtship of serener skies.—
So, six cold moons, the Dormouse charm'd to rest,
210 Indulgent Sleep! beneath thy eider breast,
In fields of Fancy climbs the kernel'd groves,
Or shares the golden harvest with his loves.—

[*Tulipa*. l. 205. Tulip. What is in common language called a bulbous root, is by Linneus termed the Hybernacle, or Winter-lodge of the young plant. As these bulbs in every respect resemble buds, except in their being produced under ground, and include the leaves and flower in miniature, which are to be expanded in the ensuing spring. By cautiously cutting in the early spring through the concentric coats of a tulip-root, longitudinally from the top to the base, and taking them off successively, the whole flower of the next summer's tulip is beautifully seen by the naked eye, with its petals, pistil, and stamens; the flowers exist in other bulbs, in the same manner, as in Hyacinths, but the individual flowers of these being less, they are not so easily differed, or so conspicuous to the naked eye.

In the seeds of the Nymphæa Nelumbo, the leaves of the plant are seen so distinctly, that Mr. Ferber found out by them to what plant the seeds belonged. Amoen. Acad. V. vi. No. 120. He says that Mariotte first observed the future flower and foliage in the bulb of a Tulip; and adds, that it is pleasant to see in the buds of the Hepatica, and Pedicularia hirsuta, yet lying in the earth; and in the gems of Daphne Mezereon; and at the base of Osmunda Lunaria, a perfect plant of the future year compleat in all its parts. Ibid.]

But bright from earth amid the troubled air
Ascends fair COLCHICA with radiant hair,
215 Warms the cold bosom of the hoary year,
And lights with Beauty's blaze the dusky sphere.

Three blushing Maids the intrepid Nymph attend,
And *six* gay Youths, enamour'd train! defend.
So shines with silver guards the Georgian star,
220 And drives on Night's blue arch his glittering car;
Hangs o'er the billowy clouds his lucid form,
Wades through the mist, and dances in the storm.

[*Colchicum autumnale*. I. 214. Autumnal Meadow-saffron. Six males, three females. The germ is buried within the root, which thus seems to constitute a part of the flower. Families of Plants, p. 242 These singular flowers appear in the autumn without any leaves, whence in some countries they are called Naked Ladies: in the March following the green leaves spring up, and in April the seed-vessel rises from the ground; the seeds ripen in May, contrary to the usual habits of vegetables, which slower in the spring, and ripen their seeds in the autumn. Miller's Dict. The juice of the root of this plant is so acrid as to produce violent effects on the human constitution, which also prevents it from being eaten by subterranean insects, and thus guards the seed-vessel during the winter. The defoliation of deciduous trees is announced by the flowering of the Colchicum; of these the ash is the last that puts forth its leaves, and the first that loses them. Phil. Bot. p. 275.

The Hamamelis, Witch Hazle, is another plant which flowers in autumn; when the leaves fall off, the flowers come out in clusters from the joints of the branches, and in Virginia ripen their seed in the ensuing spring; but in this country their seeds seldom ripen. Lin. Spec. Plant. Miller's Dict.]

Sunflower

GREAT HELIANTHUS guides o'er twilight plains
In gay solemnity his Dervise-trains;
225 Marshall'd in *fives* each gaudy band proceeds,
Each gaudy band a plumed Lady leads;
With zealous step he climbs the upland lawn,
And bows in homage to the rising dawn;
Imbibes with eagle-eye the golden ray,
230 And watches, as it moves, the orb of day.

[*Helianthus*. l. 223. Sun flower. The numerous florets, which constitute the disk of this flower, contain in each five males surrounding one female, the five stamens have their anthers connected at top, whence the name of the class "confederate males;" see note on Chondrilla. The sun-flower follows the course of the sun by nutation, not by twisting its stem. (Hales veg. stat.) Other plants, when they are confined in a room, turn the shining surface of their leaves, and bend their whole branches to the light. See Mimosa.]

[*A plumed Lady leads*. l. 226. The seeds of many plants of this class are furnished with a plume, by which admirable mechanism they are disseminated by the winds far from their parent stem, and look like a shuttlecock, as they fly. Other seeds are disseminated by animals; of these some attach themselves to their hair or feathers by a gluten, as misleto; others by hooks, as cleavers, burdock, hounds-tongue; and others are swallowed whole for the sake of the fruit, and voided uninjured, as the hawthorn, juniper, and some grasses. Other seeds again disperse themselves by means of an elastic seed-vessel, as Oats, Geranium, and Impatiens; and the seeds of aquatic plants, and of those which grow on the banks of rivers, are carried many miles by the currents, into which they fall. See Impatiens. Zostera. Cassia. Carlina.]

> Queen of the marsh, imperial DROSERA treads
> Rush-fringed banks, and moss-embroider'd beds;
> Redundant folds of glossy silk surround
> Her slender waist, and trail upon the ground;
> 235 *Five* sister-nymphs collect with graceful ease,
> Or spread the floating purple to the breeze;
> And *five* fair youths with duteous love comply
> With each soft mandate of her moving eye.
> As with sweet grace her snowy neck she bows,
> 240 A zone of diamonds trembles round her brows;
> Bright shines the silver halo, as she turns;
> And, as she steps, the living lustre burns.

[*Drosera*. l. 231. Sun-dew. Five males, five females. The leaves of this marsh-plant are purple, and have a fringe very unlike other vegetable productions. And, which is curious, at the point of every thread of this erect fringe stands a pellucid drop of mucilage, resembling a ducal coronet. This mucus is a secretion from certain glands, and like the viscous material round the flower-stalks of Silene (catchfly) prevents small insects from infesting the leaves. As the ear-wax in animals seems to be in part designed to prevent fleas and other insects from getting into their ears. See Silene. Mr. Wheatly, an eminent surgeon in Cateaton-street, London, observed these leaves to bend upwards, when an insect settled on them, like the leaves of the muscipula veneris, and pointing all their globules of mucus to the centre, that they compleatly intangled and destroyed it. M. Broussonet, in the Mem. de l'Acad. des Sciences for the year 1784. p. 615. after hiving described the motion of the Dionæa, adds, that a similar appearance has been observed in the leaves of two species of Drosera.]

[handwritten annotation: when insects get close, it moves]

> Fair LONICERA prints the dewy lawn,
> And decks with brighter blush the vermil dawn;
> 245 Winds round the shadowy rocks, and pansied vales,
> And scents with sweeter breath the summer-gales;

[*Lonicera*. l. 243. Caprifolium. Honeysuckle. Five males, one female. Nature has in many flowers used a wonderful apparatus to guard the nectary, or honey-gland, from insects. In the honey-suckle the petal terminates in a long tube like a cornucopiae, or horn of plenty; and the honey is produced at the bottom of it.

In Aconitum, monkshood, the nectaries stand upright like two horns covered with a hood, which abounds with such acrid matter that no insects penetrate it. In Helleborus, hellebore, the many nectaries are placed in a circle, like little pitchers, and add much to the beauty of the flower. In the Columbine, Aquilegia, the nectary is imagined to be like the neck and body of a bird, and the two petals standing upon each side to represent wings; whence its name of columbine, as if resembling a nest of young pigeons fluttering whilst their parent feeds them. The importance of the nectary in the economy of vegetation is explained at large in the notes on part the first.

Many insects are provided with a long and pliant proboscis for the purpose of acquiring this grateful food, as a variety of bees, moths, and butterflies: but the Sphinx Convolvuli, or unicorn moth, is furnished with the most remarkable proboscis in this climate. It carries it rolled up in concentric circles under its chin, and occasionally extends it to above three inches in length. This trunk consists of joints and muscles, and seems to have more versatile movements than the trunk of the elephant; and near its termination is split into two capillary tubes. The excellence of this contrivance for robbing the flowers of their honey, keeps this beautiful insect fat and bulky; though it flies only in the evening, when the flowers have closed their petals, and are thence more difficult of access; at the same time the brilliant colours of the moth contribute to its safety, by making it mistaken by the late sleeping birds for the flower it rests on.

Besides these there is a curious contrivance attending the Ophrys, commonly called the Bee-orchis, and the Fly-orchis, with some kinds of the Delphinium, called Bee-larkspurs, to preserve their honey; in these the nectary and petals resemble in form and colour the insects, which plunder them: and thus it may be supposed, they often escape these hourly robbers, by having the appearance of being pre-occupied. See note on Rubia, and Conserva polymorpha.]

> With artless grace and native ease she charms,
> And bears the Horn of Plenty in her arms.
> *Five* rival Swains their tender cares unfold,
> 250 And watch with eye askance the treasured gold.
>
> Where rears huge Tenerif his azure crest,
> Aspiring DRABA builds her eagle nest;
> Her pendant eyry icy caves surround,
> Where erst Volcanos min'd the rocky ground.
> 255 Pleased round the Fair *four* rival Lords ascend
> The shaggy steeps, *two* menial youths attend.
> High in the setting ray the beauty stands,
> And her tall shadow waves on distant lands.

[*Draba.* I. 252. Alpina. Alpine Whitlow-grass. One female and six males. Four of these males stand above the other two; whence the name of the class "four powers." I have observed in several plants of this class, that the two lower males arise, in a few-days after the opening of the flower, to the same height as the other four, not being mature as soon as the higher ones. See note on Gloriosa. All the plants of this class possess similar virtues; they are termed acrid and anti corbutic in their raw state, as mustard, watercress; when cultivated and boiled, they become a mild wholesome food, as cabbage, turnep.

There was formerly a Volcano on the Peake of Tenerif, which became extinct about the year 1684. Philos. Trans. In many excavations of the mountain, much below the summit, there is now found abundance of ice at all seasons. Tench's Expedition to Botany Bay, p. 12. Are these congelations in consequence of the daily solution of the hoar-frost which is produced on the summit during the night?]

Stay, bright inhabitant of air, alight,
260 Ambitious VISCA, from thy eagle-flight!—
——Scorning the sordid soil, aloft she springs,
Shakes her white plume, and claps her golden wings;
High o'er the fields of boundless ether roves,
And seeks amid the clouds her soaring loves!

265 Stretch'd on her mossy couch, in trackless deeps, Queen of the coral groves, ZOSTERA sleeps;

[*Viscum.* l. 260. Misletoe. Two houses. This plant never grows upon the ground; the foliage is yellow, and the berries milk-white; the berries are so viscous, as to serve for bird-lime; and when they fall, adhere to the branches of the tree, on which the plant grows, and strike root into its bark; or are carried to distant trees by birds. The Tillandsia, or wild pine, grows on other trees, like the Misletoe, but takes little or no nourishment from them, having large buckets in its leaves to collect and retain the rain water. See note on Dypsacus. The mosses, which grow on the bark of trees, take much nourishment from them; hence it is observed that trees, which are annually cleared from moss by a brush, grow nearly twice as fast. (Phil. Transact.) In the cyder countries the peasants brush their apple-trees annually.]

[*Zostera.* l. 266. Grass-wrack. Class, Feminine Males. Order, Many Males. It grows at the bottom of the sea, and rising to the surface, when in flower, covers many leagues; and is driven at length to the shore. During its time of floating on the sea, numberless animals live on the under surface of it; and being specifically lighter than the sea water, or being repelled by it, have legs placed as it were on their backs for the purpose of walking under it. As the Scyllcea. See Barbut's Genera Vermium. It seems necessary that the marriages of plants should be celebrated in the open air, either because the powder of the anther, or the mucilage on the stigma, or the reservoir of honey might receive injury from the water. Mr. Needham observed, that in the ripe dust of every flower, examined by the microscope, some vesicles are perceived, from which a fluid had escaped; and that those, which still retain it, explode if they be wetted, like an eolopile suddenly exposed to a strong heat. These observations have been verified by Spallanzani and others. Hence rainy seasons make a scarcity of grain, or hinder its fecundity, by bursting the pollen before it arrives at the moist stigma of the flower. Spallanzani's Dissertations, v. II. p. 321. Thus the flowers of the male Vallisneria are produced under water, and when ripe detach themselves from the plant, and rising to the surface are wafted by the air to the female flowers. See Vallisneria.]

<blockquote>
The silvery sea-weed matted round her bed,
And distant surges murmuring o'er her head.—
High in the flood her azure dome ascends,
270 The crystal arch on crystal columns bends;
Roof'd with translucent shell the turrets blaze,
And far in ocean dart their colour'd rays;
O'er the white floor successive shadows move,
As rise and break the ruffled waves above.—
275 Around the nymph her mermaid-trains repair,
And weave with orient pearl her radiant hair;
With rapid fins she cleaves the watery way,
Shoots like a silver meteor up to day;
Sounds a loud conch, convokes a scaly band,
280 Her sea-born lovers, and ascends the strand.

E'en round the pole the flames of Love aspire,
And icy bosoms feel the *secret* fire!—
Cradled in snow and fann'd by arctic air
Shines, gentle BAROMETZ! thy golden hair;
285 Rooted in earth each cloven hoof descends,
And round and round her flexile neck she bends;
Crops the grey coral moss, and hoary thyme,
Or laps with rosy tongue the melting rime;
Eyes with mute tenderness her distant dam,
290 Or seems to bleat, a *Vegetable Lamb*.
</blockquote>

[Handwritten marginal note: Legend: the plant magically turned into a little sheep.]

[*Barometz.* l. 284. Polypodium Barometz. Tartarian Lamb. Clandestine Marriage. This species of Fern is a native of China, with a decumbent root, thick, and every where covered with the most soft and dense wool, intensely yellow. Lin. Spec. Plant.

This curious stem is sometimes pushed out of the ground in its horizontal situation by some of the inferior branches of the root, so as to give it some resemblance to a Lamb standing on four legs; and has been said to destroy all other plants in its vicinity. Sir Hans Sloane describes it under the name of Tartarian Lamb, and has given a print of it. Philos. Trans. abridged, v. II. p. 646. but thinks some art had been used to give it an animal appearance. Dr. Hunter, in his edition of the Terra of Evelyn, has given a more curious print of it, much resembling a sheep. The down is used in India externally for stopping hemorrhages, and is called golden moss.

The thick downy clothing of some vegetables seems designed to protect them from the injuries of cold, like the wool of animals. Those bodies, which are bad conductors of electricity, are also bad conductors of heat, as glass, wax, air. Hence either of the two former of these may be melted by the flame of a blow-pipe very near the fingers which hold it without burning them; and the last, by being confined on the surface of animal bodies, in the interstices of their fur or wool, prevents the escape of their natural warmth; to which should be added, that the hairs themselves are imperfect conductors. The fat or oil of whales, and other northern animals, seems designed for the same purpose of preventing the too sudden escape of the heat of the body in cold climates. Snow protects vegetables which are covered by it from cold, both because it is a bad conductor of heat itself, and contains much air in its pores. If a piece of camphor be immersed in a snow-ball, except one extremity of it, on setting fire to this, as the snow melts, the water becomes absorbed into the surrounding snow by capillary attraction; on this account, when living animals are buried in snow, they are not moistened by it; but the cavity enlarges as the snow dissolves, affording them both a dry and warm habitation.]

    —So, warm and buoyant in his oily mail,
    Gambols on seas of ice the unwieldy Whale;
    Wide-waving fins round floating islands urge
    His bulk gigantic through the troubled surge;
295 With hideous yawn the flying shoals He seeks,
    Or clasps with fringe of horn his massy cheeks;
    Lifts o'er the tossing wave his nostrils bare,
    And spouts pellucid columns into air;
    The silvery arches catch the setting beams,
300 And transient rainbows tremble o'er the streams.

    Weak with nice sense, the chaste MIMOSA stands,
    From each rude touch withdraws her timid hands;
    Oft as light clouds o'er-pass the Summer-glade,
    Alarm'd she trembles at the moving shade;
305 And feels, alive through all her tender form,
    The whisper'd murmurs of the gathering storm;
    Shuts her sweet eye-lids to approaching night;
    And hails with freshen'd charms the rising light.

[*Mimosa*. I. 301. The sensitive plant. Of the class Polygamy, one house. Naturalists have not explained the immediate cause of the collapsing of the sensitive plant; the leaves meet and close in the night during the sleep of the plant, or when exposed to much cold in the day-time, in the same manner as when they are affected by external violence, folding their upper surfaces together, and in part over each other like scales or tiles; so as to expose as little of the upper surface as may be to the air; but do not indeed collapse quite so far, since I have found, when touched in the night during their sleep, they fall still further; especially when touched on the foot-stalks between the stems and the leaflets, which seems to be their most sensitive or irritable part. Now as their situation after being exposed to external violence resembles their sleep, but with a greater degree of collapse, may it not be owing to a numbness or paralysis consequent to too violent irritation, like the faintings of animals from pain or fatigue? I kept a sensitive plant in a dark room till some hours after day-break: its leaves and leaf-stalks were collapsed as in its most profound sleep, and on exposing it to the light, above twenty minutes passed before the plant was thoroughly awake and had quite expanded itself. During the night the upper or smoother surfaces of the leaves are appressed together; this would seem to shew that the office of this surface of the leaf was to expose the fluids of the plant to the light as well as to the air. See note on Helianthus. Many flowers close up their petals during the night. See note on vegetable respiration in Part I.]

> Veil'd, with gay decency and modest pride,
> 310 Slow to the mosque she moves, an eastern bride;
> There her soft vows unceasing love record,
> Queen of the bright seraglio of her Lord.—
> So sinks or rises with the changeful hour
> The liquid silver in its glassy tower.
> 315 So turns the needle to the pole it loves,
> With fine librations quivering as it moves.
>
> All wan and shivering in the leafless glade
> The sad ANEMONE reclined her head;
> Grief on her cheeks had paled the roseate hue,
> 320 And her sweet eye-lids dropp'd with pearly dew.
> —"See, from bright regions, borne on odorous gales
> The Swallow, herald of the summer, sails;

[*Anemone.* l. 318. Many males, many females. Pliny says this flower never opens its petals but when the wind blows; whence its name: it has properly no calix, but two or three sets of petals, three in each set, which are folded over the stamens and pistil in a singular and beautiful manner, and differs also from ranunculus in not having a melliferous pore on the claw of each petal.]

[*The Swallow.* l. 322. There is a wonderful conformity between the vegetation of some plants, and the arrival of certain birds of passage. Linneus observes that the wood anemone blows in Sweden on the arrival of the swallow; and the marsh mary-gold, Caltha, when the cuckoo sings. Near the same coincidence was observed in England by Stillingfleet. The word Coccux in Greek signifies both a young fig and a cuckoo, which is supposed to have arisen from the coincidence of their appearance in Greece. Perhaps a similar coincidence of appearance in some parts of Asia gave occasion to the story of the loves of the rose and nightingale, so much celebrated by the eastern poets. See Dianthus. The times however of the appearance of vegetables in the spring seem occasionally to be influenced by their acquired habits, as well as by their sensibility to heat: for the roots of potatoes, onions, &c. will germinate with much less heat in the spring than in the autumn; as is easily observable where these roots are stored for use; and hence malt is best made in the spring. 2d. The grains and roots brought from more southern latitudes germinate here sooner than those which are brought from more northern ones, owing to their acquired habits. Fordyce on Agriculture. 3d. It was observed by one of the scholars of Linneus, that the apple-trees sent from hence to New England blossomed for a few years too early for that climate, and bore no fruit; but afterwards learnt to accommodate themselves to their new situation. (Kalm's Travels.) 4th. The parts of animals become more sensible to heat after having been previously exposed to cold, as our hands glow on coming into the house after having held snow in them; this seems to happen to vegetables; for vines in grape-houses, which have been exposed to the winter's cold, will become forwarder and more vigorous than those which have been kept during the winter in the house. (Kenedy on Gardening.) This accounts for the very rapid vegetation in the northern latitudes after the solution of the snows.

The increase of the irritability of plants in respect to heat, after having been previously exposed to cold, is further illustrated by an experiment of Dr. Walker's. He cut apertures into a birch-tree at different heights; and on the 26th of March some of these apertures bled, or oozed with the sap-juice, when the thermometer was at 39; which same apertures did not bleed on the 13th of March, when the thermometer was at 44. The reason of this I apprehend was, because on the night of the 25th the thermometer was as low as 34; whereas on the night of the 12th it was at 41; though the ingenious author ascribes it to another cause. Trans. of Royal Soc. of Edinburgh, v. 1. p. 19.]

"Breathe, gentle AIR! from cherub-lips impart
Thy balmy influence to my anguish'd heart;
325 Thou, whose soft voice calls forth the tender blooms,
Whose pencil paints them, and whose breath perfumes;
O chase the Fiend of Frost, with leaden mace
Who seals in death-like sleep my hapless race;
Melt his hard heart, release his iron hand,
330 And give my ivory petals to expand.
So may each bud, that decks the brow of spring,
Shed all its incense on thy wafting wing!"—

To her fond prayer propitious Zephyr yields,
Sweeps on his sliding shell through azure fields,
335 O'er her fair mansion waves his whispering wand,
And gives her ivory petals to expand;

Gives with new life her filial train to rise,
And hail with kindling smiles the genial skies.
So shines the Nymph in beauty's blushing pride,
340 When Zephyr wafts her deep calash aside;
Tears with rude kiss her bosom's gauzy veil,
And flings the fluttering kerchief to the gale.
So bright, the folding canopy undrawn,
Glides the gilt Landau o'er the velvet lawn,
345 Of beaux and belles displays the glittering throng;
And soft airs fan them, as they roll along.

Where frowning Snowden bends his dizzy brow
O'er Conway, listening to the surge below;
Retiring LICHEN climbs the topmost stone,
350 And 'mid the airy ocean dwells alone.—
Bright shine the stars unnumber'd *o'er her head*,
And the cold moon-beam gilds her flinty bed;
While round the rifted rocks hoarse whirlwinds breathe,
And dark with thunder sail the clouds *beneath.*—
355 The steepy path her plighted swain pursues,
And tracks her light step o'er th' imprinted dews,
Delighted Hymen gives his torch to blaze,
Winds round the craggs, and lights the mazy ways;

[*Lichen*. l. 349. Calcareum. Liver-wort. Clandestine Marriage. This plant is the first that vegetates on naked rocks, covering them with a kind of tapestry, and draws its nourishment perhaps chiefly from the air; after it perishes, earth enough is left for other mosses to root themselves; and after some ages a soil is produced sufficient for the growth of more succulent and large vegetables. In this manner perhaps the whole earth has been gradually covered with vegetation, after it was raised out of the primeval ocean by subterraneous fires.]

Sheds o'er their *secret* vows his influence chaste, 360 And decks with roses the admiring waste.

High in the front of heaven when Sirius glares,
And o'er Britannia shakes his fiery hairs;
When no soft shower descends, no dew distills,
Her wave-worn channels dry, and mute her rills;
365 When droops the sickening herb, the blossom fades,
And parch'd earth gapes beneath the withering glades.
—With languid step fair DYPSACA retreats;
"Fall gentle dews!" the fainting nymph repeats;
Seeks the low dell, and in the sultry shade
370 Invokes in vain the Naiads to her aid.—

[*Dypsacus*. l. 367. Teasel. One female, and four males. There is a cup around every joint of the stem of this plant, which contains from a spoonful to half a pint of water; and serves both for the nutriment of the plant in dry seasons, and to prevent insects from creeping up to devour its seed. See Silene. The Tillandsia, or wild pine, of the West Indies has every leaf terminated near the stalk with a hollow bucket, which contains from half a pint to a quart of water. Dampier's Voyage to Campeachy. Dr. Sloane mentions one kind of aloe furnished with leaves, which, like the wild pine and Banana, hold water; and thence afford necessary refreshment to travellers in hot countries. Nepenthes had a bucket for the same purpose at the end of every leaf, Burm. Zeyl. 41. 17.]

> *Four* silvan youths in crystal goblets bear
> The untasted treasure to the grateful fair;
> Pleased from their hands with modest grace she sips,
> And the cool wave reflects her coral lips.

375   With nice selection modest RUBIA blends,
> Her vermil dyes, and o'er the cauldron bends;
> Warm 'mid the rising steam the Beauty glows,
> As blushes in a mist the dewy rose.

[*Rubia*. l. 375. Madder. Four males and one female. This plant is cultivated in very large quantities for dying red. If mixed with the food of young pigs or chickens, it colours their bones red. If they are fed alternate fortnights with a mixture of madder, and with their usual food alone, their bones will consist of concentric circles of white and red. Belchier. Phil. Trans. 1736. Animals fed with madder for the purpose of these experiments were found upon dissection to have thinner gall. Comment. de rebus. Lipsiæ. This circumstance is worth further attention. The colouring materials of vegetables, like those which serve the purpose of tanning, varnishing, and the various medical purposes, do not seem essential to the life of the plant; but seem given it as a defence against the depredations of insects or other animals, to whom these materials are nauseous or deleterious. To insects and many smaller animals their colours contribute to conceal them from the larger ones which prey upon them. Caterpillars which feed on leaves are generally green; and earth-worms the colour of the earth which they inhabit; Butterflies which frequent flowers, are coloured like them; small birds which frequent hedges have greenish backs like the leaves, and light coloured bellies like the sky, and are hence less visible to the hawk, who passes under them or over them. Those birds which are much amongst flowers, as the gold-finch (Fringilla carduelis), are furnished with vivid colours. The lark, partridge, hare, are the colour of the dry vegetables or earth on which they rest. And frogs vary their colour with the mud of the streams which they frequent; and those which live on trees are green. Fish, which are generally suspended in water, and swallows, which are generally suspended in air, have their backs the colour of the distant ground, and their bellies of the sky. In the colder climates many of these become white during the existence of the snows. Hence there is apparent design in the colours of animals, whilst those of vegetables seem consequent to the other properties of the materials which possess them.]

With chemic art *four* favour'd youths aloof
380 Stain the white fleece, or stretch the tinted woof;
O'er Age's cheek the warmth of youth diffuse,
Or deck the pale-eyed nymph in roseate hues.
So when MEDEA to exulting Greece
From plunder'd COLCHIS bore the golden fleece;
385 On the loud shore a magic pile she rais'd,
The cauldron bubbled, and the faggots blaz'd;—
Pleased on the boiling wave old ÆSON swims,
And feels new vigour stretch his swelling limbs;

[*Pleased on the boiling wave.* l. 387. The story of Æson becoming young, from the medicated bath of Medea, seems to have been intended to teach the efficacy of warm bathing in retarding the progress of old age. The words *relaxation and bracing*, which are generally thought expressive of the effects of warm and cold bathing, are mechanical terms, properly applied to drums or strings; but are only metaphors when applied to the effects of cold or warm bathing on animal bodies. The immediate cause of old age seems to reside in the inirritability of the finer vessels or parts of our system; hence these cease to act, and collapse or become horny or bony. The warm bath is peculiarly adapted to prevent these circumstances by its increasing our irritability, and by moistening and softening the skin, and the extremities of the finer vessels, which terminate in it. To those who are past the meridian of life, and have dry skins, and begin to be emaciated, the warm bath, for half an hour twice a week, I believe to be eminently serviceable in retarding the advances of age.]

Through his thrill'd nerves forgotten ardors dart,
390 And warmer eddies circle round his heart;
With softer fires his kindling eye-balls glow,
And darker tresses wanton round his brow.

As dash the waves on India's breezy strand,
Her flush'd cheek press'd upon her lily hand,
395 VALLISNER sits, up-turns her tearful eyes,
Calls her lost lover, and upbraids the skies;

[*Vallisniria.* l. 395. This extraordinary plant is of the class Two Houses. It is found in the East Indies, in Norway, and various parts of Italy. Lin. Spec. Plant. They have their roots at the bottom of the Rhone, the flowers of the female plant float on the surface of the water, and are furnished with an elastic spiral stalk, which extends or contracts as the water rises and falls; this rise or fall, from the rapid descent of the river, and the mountain torrents which flow into it, often amounts to many feet in a few hours. The flowers of the male plant are produced under water, and as soon as their farina, or dust, is mature; they detach themselves from the plant, and rise to the surface, continue to flourish, and are wafted by the air, or borne by the currents to the female flowers. In this resembling those tribes of insects, where the males at certain seasons acquire wings, but not the females, as ants, Cocchus, Lampyris, Phalæna, Brumata, Lichanella. These male flowers are in such numbers, though very minute, as frequently to cover the surface of the river to considerable extent. See Families of Plants translated from Linneus, p. 677.]

> For him she breathes the silent sigh, forlorn,
> Each setting-day; for him each rising morn.—
> "Bright orbs, that light yon high etherial plain,
> 400 Or bathe your radiant tresses in the main;
> Pale moon, that silver'st o'er night's sable brow;—
> For ye were witness to his parting vow!—
> Ye shelving rocks, dark waves, and sounding shore,—
> Ye echoed sweet the tender words he swore!—
> 405 Can stars or seas the sails of love retain?
> O guide my wanderer to my arms again!"—

> Her buoyant skiff intrepid ULVA guides,
> And seeks her Lord amid the trackless tides;

[*Ulva*, l. 407. Clandestine marriage. This kind of sea-weed is buoyed up by bladders of air, which are formed in the duplicatures of its leaves; and forms immense floating fields of vegetation; the young ones, branching out from the larger ones, and borne on similar little air-vessels. It is also found in the warm baths of Patavia; where the leaves are formed into curious cells or labyrinths for the purpose of floating on the water. See ulva labyrinthi-formis Lin. Spec. Plant. The air contained in these cells was found by Dr. Priestley to be sometimes purer than common air, and sometimes less pure; the air-bladders of fish seem to be similar organs, and serve to render them buoyant in the water. In some of these, as in the Cod and Haddock, a red membrane, consisting of a great number of leaves or duplicatures, is found within the air-bag, which probably secretes this air from the blood of the animal. (Monro. Physiol. of Fish. p. 28.) To determine whether this air, when first separated from the blood of the animal or plant, be dephlogisticated air, is worthy inquiry. The bladder-sena (Colutea), and bladder-nut (Staphylæa), have their seed-vessels distended with air; the Ketmia has the upper joint of the stem immediately under the receptacle of the flower much distended with air; these seem to be analogous to the air-vessel at the broad end of the egg, and may probably become less pure as the seed ripens: some, which I tried, had the purity of the surrounding atmosphere. The air at the broad end of the egg is probably an organ serving the purpose of respiration to the young chick, some of whose vessels are spread upon it like a placenta, or permeate it. Many are of opinion that even the placenta of the human fetus, and cotyledons of quadrupeds, are respiratory organs rather than nutritious ones.

The air in the hollow stems of grasses, and of some umbelliferous plants, bears analogy to the air in the quills, and in some of the bones of birds; supplying the place of the pith, which shrivels up after it has performed its office of protruding the young stem or feather. Some of these cavities of the bones are said to communicate with the lungs in birds. Phil. Trans.

The air-bladders of fish are nicely adapted to their intended purpose; for though they render them buoyant near the surface without the labour of using their fins, yet, when they rest at greater depths, they are no inconvenience, as the increased pressure of the water condenses the air which they contain into less space. Thus, if a cork or bladder of air was immersed a very great depth in the ocean, it would be so much compressed, as to become specifically as heavy as the water, and would remain there. It is probable the unfortunate Mr. Day, who was drowned in a diving-ship of his own construction, miscarried from not attending to this circumstance: it is probable the quantity of air he took down with him, if he descended much lower than he expected, was condensed into so small a space as not to render the ship buoyant when he endeavoured to ascend.]

Her *secret* vows the Cyprian Queen approves,
410 And hovering halcyons guard her infant-loves;
     Each in his floating cradle round they throng,
     And dimpling Ocean bears the fleet along.—
     Thus o'er the waves, which gently bend and swell,
     Fair GALATEA steers her silver shell;

415 Her playful Dolphins stretch the silken rein,
     Hear her sweet voice, and glide along the main.
     As round the wild meandering coast she moves
     By gushing rills, rude cliffs, and nodding groves;
     Each by her pine the Wood-nymphs wave their locks,
420 And wondering Naiads peep amid the rocks;
     Pleased trains of Mermaids rise from coral cells,
     Admiring Tritons sound their twisted shells;
     Charm'd o'er the car pursuing Cupids sweep,
     Their snow-white pinions twinkling in the deep;
425 And, as the lustre of her eye she turns,
     Soft sighs the Gale, and amorous Ocean burns.

     On DOVE'S green brink the fair TREMELLA stood,
     And view'd her playful image in the flood;

[*Tremella*, l. 427. Clandestine marriage. I have frequently observed fungusses of this Genus on old rails and on the ground to become a transparent jelly, after they had been frozen in autumnal mornings; which is a curious property, and distinguishes them from some other vegetable mucilage; for I have observed that the paste, made by boiling wheat-flour in water, ceases to be adhesive after having been frozen. I suspected that the Tremella Nostoc, or star-jelly, also had been thus produced; but have since been well informed, that the Tremella Nostoc is a mucilage voided by Herons after they have eaten frogs; hence it has the appearance of having been pressed through a hole; and limbs of frogs are said sometimes to be found amongst it; it is always seen upon plains or by the sides of water, places which Herons generally frequent.

Some of the Fungusses are so acrid, that a drop of their juice blisters the tongue; others intoxicate those who eat them. The Ostiacks in Siberia use them for the latter purpose; one Fungus of the species, Agaricus muscarum, eaten raw; or the decoction of three of them, produces intoxication for 12 or 16 hours. History of Russia. V. 1. Nichols. 1780. As all acrid plants become less so, if exposed to a boiling heat, it is probable the common mushroom may sometimes disagree from being not sufficiently stewed. The Oftiacks blister their skin by a fungus found on Birch-trees; and use the Agiricus officin. for Soap. ib.

There was a dispute whether the fungusses should be classed in the animal or vegetable department. Their animal taste in cookery, and their animal smell when burnt, together with their tendency to putrefaction, insomuch that the Phallus impudicus has gained the name of stink-horn; and lastly, their growing and continuing healthy without light, as the Licoperdon tuber or truffle, and the fungus vinosus or mucor in dark cellars, and the esculent mushrooms on beds covered thick with straw, would seem to shew that they approach towards the animals, or make a kind of isthmus connecting the two mighty kingdoms of animal and of vegetable nature.]

      To each rude rock, lone dell, and echoing grove
430 Sung the sweet sorrows of her *secret* love.
      "Oh, stay!—return!"—along the sounding shore
      Cry'd the sad Naiads,—she return'd no more!—
      Now girt with clouds the sullen Evening frown'd,
      And withering Eurus swept along the ground;
435 The misty moon withdrew her horned light,
      And sunk with Hesper in the skirt of night;

      No dim electric streams, (the northern dawn,)
      With meek effulgence quiver'd o'er the lawn;
      No star benignant shot one transient ray
440 To guide or light the wanderer on her way.
      Round the dark craggs the murmuring whirlwinds blow,
      Woods groan above, and waters roar below;
      As o'er the steeps with pausing foot she moves,

The pitying Dryads shriek amid their groves;
445 She flies,—she stops,—she pants—she looks behind,
And hears a demon howl in every wind.
—As the bleak blast unfurls her fluttering vest,
Cold beats the snow upon her shuddering breast;
Through her numb'd limbs the chill sensations dart,
450 And the keen ice bolt trembles at her heart.
"I sink, I fall! oh, help me, help!" she cries,
Her stiffening tongue the unfinish'd sound denies;
Tear after tear adown her cheek succeeds,
And pearls of ice bestrew the glittering meads;
455 Congealing snows her lingering feet surround,
Arrest her flight, and root her to the ground;
With suppliant arms she pours the silent prayer;
Her suppliant arms hang crystal in the air;
Pellucid films her shivering neck o'erspread,
460 Seal her mute lips, and silver o'er her head,
Veil her pale bosom, glaze her lifted hands,
And shrined in ice the beauteous statue stands.
—DOVE'S azure nymphs on each revolving year
For fair TREMELLA shed the tender tear;
465 With rush-wove crowns in sad procession move,
And sound the sorrowing shell to hapless love."

Here paused the MUSE,—across the darken'd pole
Sail the dim clouds, the echoing thunders roll;
The trembling Wood-nymphs, as the tempest lowers,
470 Lead the gay Goddess to their inmost bowers;
Hang the mute lyre the laurel shade beneath,
And round her temples bind the myrtle wreath.
—Now the light swallow with her airy brood
Skims the green meadow, and the dimpled flood;
475 Loud shrieks the lone thrush from his leafless thorn,
Th' alarmed beetle sounds his bugle horn;
Each pendant spider winds with fingers fine
His ravel'd clue, and climbs along the line;
Gay Gnomes in glittering circles stand aloof
480 Beneath a spreading mushroom's fretted roof;
Swift bees returning seek their waxen cells,
And Sylphs cling quivering in the lily's bells.
Through the still air descend the genial showers,
And pearly rain-drops deck the laughing flowers.

INTERLUDE.

Poetry vs. Prose

Bookseller. Your verses, Mr. Botanist, consist of *pure description*, I hope there is *sense* in the notes.

Poet. I am only a flower-painter, or occasionally attempt a landskip; and leave the human figure with the subjects of history to abler artists.

B. It is well to know what subjects are within the limits of your pencil; many have failed of success from the want of this self-knowledge. But pray tell me, what is the essential difference between Poetry and Prose? is it solely the melody or measure of the language?

P. I think not solely; for some prose has its melody, and even measure. And good verses, well spoken in a language unknown to the hearer, are not easily to be distinguished from good prose. *B.* Is it the sublimity, beauty, or novelty of the sentiments?

P. Not so; for sublime sentiments are often better expressed in prose. Thus when Warwick in one of the plays of Shakespear, is left wounded on the field after the loss of the battle, and his friend says to him, "Oh, could you but fly!" what can be more sublime than his answer, "Why then, I would not fly." No measure of verse, I imagine, could add dignity to this sentiment. And it would be easy to select examples of the beautiful or new from prose writers, which I suppose no measure of verse could improve.

B. In what then consists the essential difference between Poetry and Prose?

P. Next to the measure of the language, the principal distinction appears to me to consist in this: that Poetry admits of but few words expressive of very abstracted ideas, whereas Prose abounds with them. And as our ideas derived from visible objects are more distinct than those derived from the objects of our other senses, the words expressive of these ideas belonging to vision make up the principal part of poetic language. That is, the Poet writes principally to the eye, the Prose-writer uses more abstracted terms. Mr. Pope has written a bad verse in the Windsor Forest:

"And Kennet swift for silver Eels *renown'd.*"

The word renown'd does not present the idea of a visible object to the mind, and is thence prosaic. But change this line thus,

"And Kennet swift, where silver Graylings *play.*" and it becomes poetry, because the scenery is then brought before the eye.

B. This may be done in prose.

P. And when it is done in a single word, it animates the prose; so it is more agreeable to read in Mr. Gibbon's History, "Germany was at this time *over-shadowed* with extensive forests;" than Germany was at this time *full* of extensive forests. But where this mode of expression occurs too frequently, the prose approaches to poetry: and in graver works, where we expect to be instructed rather than amused, it becomes tedious and impertinent. Some parts of Mr. Burke's eloquent orations become intricate and enervated by superfluity of poetic ornament; which quantity of ornament would have been agreeable in a poem, where much ornament is expected.

B. Is then the office of poetry only to amuse?

P. The Muses are young ladies, we expect to see them dressed; though not like some modern beauties with so much gauze and feather, that "the Lady herself is the least part of her." There are however didactic pieces of poetry, which are much admired, as the Georgics of Virgil, Mason's English Garden, Hayley's Epistles; nevertheless Science is best delivered in Prose, as its mode of reasoning is from stricter analogies than metaphors or similies.

B. Do not Personifications and Allegories distinguish poetry?

P. These are other arts of bringing objects before the eye; or of expressing sentiments in the language of vision; and are indeed better suited to the pen than the pencil.

B. That is strange, when you have just said they are used to bring their objects before the eye.

P. In poetry the personification or allegoric figure is generally indistinct, and therefore does not strike us as forcibly as to make us attend to its improbability; but in painting, the figures being all much more distinct, their improbability becomes apparent, and seizes our attention to it. Thus the person of Concealment is very indistinct and therefore does not compel us to attend to its improbability, in the following beautiful lines of Shakespear:

> "—She never told her love;
> But let Concealment, like a worm i' th' bud,
> Feed on her damask cheek."—

shakespear's 12th Night

But in these lines below the person of Reason obtrudes itself into our company, and becomes disagreeable by its distinctness, and consequent improbability.

> "To Reason I flew, and intreated her aid,
> Who paused on my case, and each circumstance weigh'd;
> Then gravely reply'd in return to my prayer,
> That Hebe was fairest of all that were fair.
> That's a truth, reply'd I, I've no need to be taught,
> I came to you, Reason, to find out a fault.
> If that's all, says Reason, return as you came,
> To find fault with Hebe would forfeit my name."

Allegoric figures are on this account in general less manageable in painting and in statuary than in poetry: and can seldom be introduced in the two former arts in company with natural figures, as is evident from the ridiculous effect of many of the paintings of Rubens in the Luxemburgh gallery; and for this reason, because their improbability becomes more striking, when there are the figures of real persons by their side to compare them with. Mrs. Angelica Kauffman, well apprised of this circumstance, has introduced no mortal figures amongst her Cupids and her Graces. And the great Roubiliac, in his unrivalled monument of Time and Fame struggling for the trophy of General Fleming, has only hung up a medallion of the head of the hero of the piece. There are however some allegoric figures, which we have so often heard described or seen delineated, that we almost forget that they do not exist in common life; and hence view them without astonishment; as the figures of the heathen mythology, of angels, devils, death and time; and almost believe them to be realities, even when they are mixed with representations of the natural forms of man. Whence I conclude, that a certain degree of probability is necessary to prevent us from revolting with distaste from unnatural images; unless we are otherwise so much interested in the contemplation of them as not to perceive their improbability.

B. Is this reasoning about degrees of probability just?—When Sir Joshua Reynolds, who is unequalled both in the theory and practice of his art, and who is a great master of the pen as well as the pencil, has asserted in a discourse delivered to the Royal Academy, December 11, 1786, that "the higher styles of painting, like the higher kinds of the Drama, do not aim at any thing like deception; or have any expectation, that the spectators should think the events there represented are really passing before them." And he then accuses Mr. Fielding of bad judgment, when he attempts to compliment Mr. Garrick in one of his novels, by introducing an ignorant man, mistaking the representation of a scene in Hamlet for a reality; and thinks, because he was an ignorant man, he was less liable to make such a mistake.

P. It is a metaphysical question, and requires more attention than Sir Joshua has bestowed upon it.—You will allow, that we are perfectly deceived in our dreams; and that even in our waking reveries, we are often so much absorbed in the contemplation of what passes in our imaginations, that for a while we do not attend to the lapse of time or to our own locality; and thus suffer a similar kind of deception as in our dreams. That is, we believe things present before our eyes, which are not so.

There are two circumstances, which contribute to this compleat deception in our dreams. First, because in sleep the organs of sense are closed or inert, and hence the trains of ideas associated in our imaginations are never interrupted or dissevered by the irritations of external objects, and can not therefore be contrasted with our sensations. On this account, though we are affected with a variety of passions in our dreams, as anger, love, joy; yet we never experience surprize.—For surprize is only produced when any external irritations suddenly obtrude themselves, and dissever our passing trains of ideas.

Secondly, because in sleep there is a total suspension of our voluntary power, both over the muscles of our bodies, and the ideas of our minds; for we neither walk about, nor reason in compleat sleep. Hence, as the trains of ideas are passing in our imaginations in dreams, we cannot compare them with our previous knowledge of things, as we do in our waking hours; for this is a voluntary exertion; and thus we cannot perceive their incongruity. Thus we are deprived in sleep of the only two means by which we can distinguish the trains of ideas passing in our imaginations, from those excited by our sensations; and are led by their vivacity to believe them to belong to the latter. For the vivacity of these trains of ideas, passing in the imagination, is greatly increased by the causes above-mentioned; that is, by their not being disturbed or dissevered either by the appulses of external bodies, as in surprize; or by our voluntary exertions in comparing them with our previous knowledge, of things, as in reasoning upon them.

B. Now to apply.

P. When by the art of the Painter or Poet a train of ideas is suggested to our imaginations, which interests us so much by the pain or pleasure it affords, that we cease to attend to the irritations of common external objects, and cease also to use any voluntary efforts to compare these interesting trains of ideas with our previous knowledge of things, a compleat reverie is produced: during which time, however short, if it be but for a moment, the objects themselves appear to exist before us. This, I think, has been called by an ingenious critic "the ideal presence" of such objects. (Elements of Criticism by Lord Kaimes). And in respect to the compliment intended by Mr. Fielding to Mr. Garrick, it would seem that an ignorant Rustic at the play of Hamlet, who has some previous belief in the appearance of Ghosts, would sooner be liable to fall into reverie, and continue in it longer, than one who possessed more knowledge of the real nature of things, and had a greater facility of exercising his reason.

B. It must require great art in the Painter or Poet to produce this kind of deception?

P. The matter must be interesting from its sublimity, beauty, or novelty; this is the scientific part; and the art consists in bringing these distinctly before the eye, so as to produce (as above-mentioned) the ideal presence of the object, in which the great Shakespear particularly excells.

B. Then it is not of any consequence whether the representations correspond with nature?

P. Not if they so much interest the reader or spectator as to induce the reverie above described. Nature may be seen in the market-place, or at the card-table; but we expect something more than this in the play-house or picture-room. The further the artists recedes from nature, the greater novelty he is likely to produce; if he rises above nature, he produces the sublime; and beauty is probably a selection and new combination of her most agreeable parts. Yourself will be sensible of the truth of this doctrine by recollecting over in your mind the works of three of our celebrated artists. Sir Joshua Reynolds has introduced sublimity even into its portraits; we admire the representation of persons, whose reality we should have passed by unnoticed. Mrs. Angelica Kauffman attracts our eyes with beauty, which I suppose no where exists; certainly few Grecian faces are seen in this country. And the daring pencil of Fuseli transports us beyond the boundaries of nature, and ravishes us with the charm of the most interesting novelty. And Shakespear, who excells in all these together, so far captivates the spectator, as to make him unmindful of every kind of violation of Time, Place, or Existence. As at the first appearance of the Ghost of Hamlet, "his ear must be dull as the fat weed, which roots itself on Lethe's brink," who can attend to the improbablity of the exhibition. So in many scenes of the Tempest we perpetually believe the action passing before our eyes, and relapse with somewhat of distaste into common life at the intervals of the representation.

B. I suppose a poet of less ability would find such great machinery difficult and cumbersome to manage?

P. Just so, we should be mocked at the apparent improbabilities. As in the gardens of a Sicilian nobleman, described in Mr. Brydone's and in Mr. Swinburn's travels, there are said to be six hundred statues of imaginary monsters, which so disgust the spectators, that the state had once a serious design of destroying them; and yet the very improbable monsters in Ovid's Metamorphoses have entertained the world for many centuries.

B. The monsters in your Botanic Garden, I hope, are of the latter kind?

P. The candid reader must determine.

42

THE LOVES OF THE PLANTS.

CANTO II.

Again the Goddess strikes the golden lyre,
And tunes to wilder notes the warbling wire;
With soft suspended step Attention moves,
And Silence hovers o'er the listening groves;
5   Orb within orb the charmed audience throng,
And the green vault reverberates the song.
"Breathe soft, ye Gales!" the fair CARLINA cries,
Bear on broad wings your Votress to the skies.
How sweetly mutable yon orient hues,
10   As Morn's fair hand her opening roses strews;
How bright, when Iris blending many a ray
Binds in embroider'd wreath the brow of Day;
Soft, when the pendant Moon with lustres pale
O'er heaven's blue arch unfurls her milky veil;
15   While from the north long threads of silver light
Dart on swift shuttles o'er the tissued night!

[*Carlina*. l. 7. Carline Thistle. Of the class Confederate Males. The seeds of this and of many other plants of the same class are furnished with a plume, by which admirable mechanism they perform long aerial journeys, crossing lakes and deserts, and are thus disseminated far from the original plant, and have much the appearance of a Shuttlecock as they fly. The wings are of different construction, some being like a divergent tuft of hairs, others are branched like feathers, some are elevated from the crown of the seed by a slender foot-stalk, which gives, than a very elegant appearance, others sit immediately on the crown of the seed.

Nature has many other curious vegetable contrivances for the dispersion of seeds: see note on Helianthus. But perhaps none of them has more the appearance of design than the admirable apparatus of Tillandsia for this purpose. This plant grows on the branches of trees, like the misleto, and never on the ground; the seeds are furnished with many long threads on their crowns; which, as they are driven forwards by the winds, wrap round the arms of trees, and thus hold them fast till they vegetate. This it very analogous to the migration of Spiders on the gossamer, who are said to attach themselves to the end of a long thread, and rise thus to the tops of trees or buildings, as the accidental breezes carry them.]

"Breathe soft, ye Zephyrs! hear my fervent sighs,
Bear on broad wings your Votress to the skies!"—
—Plume over plume in long divergent lines
20   On whale-bone ribs the fair Mechanic joins;

Inlays with eider down the silken strings,
And weaves in wide expanse Dædalian wings;
Round her bold sons the waving pennons binds,
And walks with angel-step upon the winds.

25   So on the shoreless air the intrepid Gaul
Launch'd the vast concave of his buoyant ball.—
Journeying on high, the silken castle glides
Bright as a meteor through the azure tides;
O'er towns and towers and temples wins its way,
30   Or mounts sublime, and gilds the vault of day.
Silent with upturn'd eyes unbreathing crowds
Pursue the floating wonder to the clouds;
And, flush'd with transport or benumb'd with fear,
Watch, as it rises, the diminish'd sphere.
35   —Now less and less!—and now a speck is seen!—
And now the fleeting rack obtrudes between!—
With bended knees, raised arms, and suppliant brow
To every shrine with mingled cries they vow.—
"Save Him, ye Saints! who o'er the good preside;
40   "Bear Him, ye Winds! ye Stars benignant! guide."
—The calm Philosopher in ether sails,
Views broader stars, and breathes in purer gales;
Sees, like a map, in many a waving line
Round Earth's blue plains her lucid water shine;
45   Sees at his feet the forky lightnings glow,
And hears innocuous thunders roar below.—
——Rise, great MONGOLFIER! urge thy venturous flight
High o'er the Moon's pale ice-reflected light;
High o'er the pearly Star, whose beamy horn.
50   Hangs in the east, gay harbinger of morn;
Leave the red eye of Mars on rapid wing;
Jove's silver guards, and Saturn's dusky ring;
Leave the fair beams, which, issuing from afar;
Play with new lustres round the Georgian star;
55   Shun with strong oars the Sun's attractive throne,
The sparkling zodiack, and the milky zone;
Where headlong Comets with increasing force
Through other systems bend their blazing course.—
For thee Cassiope her chair withdraws,
60   For thee the Bear retracts his shaggy paws;
High o'er the North thy golden orb shall roll,
And blaze eternal round the wondering pole.
So Argo, rising from the southern main,
Lights with new stars the blue etherial plain;

[handwritten annotation: hot air balloon. carried by the wind like the Carlina]

65   With favoring beams the mariner protects,
    And the bold course, which first it steer'd, directs.

Inventress of the Woof, fair LINA flings
    The flying shuttle through the dancing strings;

[*For thee the Bear.* l. 60. Tibi jam brachia contrahit ardens Scorpius. Virg. Georg. l. 1. 34. A new star appeared in Cassiope's chair in 1572. Herschel's Construction of the Heavens. Phil. Trans. V. 75. p. 266.]

[*Linum.* l. 67. Flax Five males and five females. It was first found on the banks of the Nile. The Linum Lusitanicum, or portigal flax, has ten males: see the note on Curcuma. Isis was said to invent spinning and weaving: mankind before that time were clothed with the skins of animals. The fable of Arachne was to compliment this new art of spinning and weaving, supposed to surpass in fineness the web of the Spider.]

    Inlays the broider'd weft with flowery dyes,
70   Quick beat the reeds, the pedals fall and rise;
    Slow from the beam the lengths of warp unwind,
    And dance and nod the massy weights behind.—
    Taught by her labours, from the fertile soil
    Immortal Isis clothed the banks of Nile;
75   And fair ARACHNE with her rival loom
    Found undeserved a melancholy doom.—
    Five Sister-nymphs with dewy fingers twine
    The beamy flax, and stretch the fibre-line;
    Quick eddying threads from rapid spindles reel,
80   Or whirl with beaten foot the dizzy wheel.
    —Charm'd round the busy Fair *five* shepherds press,
    Praise the nice texture of their snowy dress,
    Admire the Artists, and the art approve,
    And tell with honey'd words the tale of love.

85   So now, where Derwent rolls his dusky floods
    Through vaulted mountains, and a night of woods,
    The Nymph, GOSSYPIA, treads the velvet sod,
    And warms with rosy smiles the watery God;
    His ponderous oars to slender spindles turns,
90   And pours o'er massy wheels his foamy urns;
    With playful charms her hoary lover wins,
    And wields his trident,—while the Monarch spins,
    —First with nice eye emerging Naiads cull
    From leathery pods the vegetable wool;

[*Gossypia*. l. 87. Gossypium. The cotton plant. On the river Derwent near Matlock in Derbyshire, Sir RICHARD ARKWRIGHT has created his curious and magnificent machinery for spinning cotton; which had been in vain attempted by many ingenious artists before him. The cotton-wool is first picked from the pods and seeds by women. It is then carded by *cylindrical cards*, which move against each other, with different velocities. It is taken from these by an *iron-hand* or comb, which has a motion similar to that of scratching, and takes the wool off the cards longitudinally in respect to the fibres or staple, producing a continued line loosely cohering, called the *Rove* or *Roving*. This Rove, yet very loosely twisted, is then received or drawn into a *whirling canister*, and is rolled by the centrifugal force in spiral lines within it; being yet too tender for the spindle. It is then passed between *two pairs of rollers*; the second pair moving faster than the first elongate the thread with greater equality than can be done by the hand; and is then twisted on spoles or bobbins.

The great fertility of the Cotton-plant in these fine flexile threads, whilst those from Flax, Hemp, and Nettles, or from the bark of the Mulberry-tree, require a previous putrefection of the parenchymatous substance, and much mechanical labour, and afterwards bleaching, renders this plant of great importance to the world. And since Sir Richard Arkwright's ingenious machine has not only greatly abbreviated and simplefied the labour and art of carding and spinning the Cotton-wool, but performs both these circumstances *better* than can be done by hand, it is probable, that the clothing of this small seed will become the principal clothing of mankind; though animal wool and silk may be preferable in colder climates, as they are more imperfect conductors of heat, and are thence a warmer clothing.]

> 95 With wiry teeth *revolving cards* release
>   The tangled knots, and smooth the ravell'd fleece;
>   Next moves the *iron-hand* with fingers fine,
>   Combs the wide card, and forms the eternal line;
>   Slow, with soft lips, the *whirling Can* acquires
> 100 The tender skeins, and wraps in rising spires;
>   With quicken'd pace *successive rollers* move,
>   And these retain, and those extend the *rove*;
>   Then fly the spoles, the rapid axles glow;—
>   And slowly circumvolves the labouring wheel below. ✶
>   wind, twist around
> 105 PAPYRA, throned upon the banks of Nile,
>   Spread her smooth leaf, and waved her silver style.

[*Cyperus. Papyrus*. l. 105. Three males, one female. The leaf of this plant was first used for paper, whence the word *paper*; and leaf, or folium, for a fold of a book. Afterwards the bark of a species of mulberry was used; whence *liber* signifies a book, and the bark of a tree. Before the invention of letters mankind may be said to have been perpetually in their infancy, as the arts of one age or

46

country generally died with their inventors. Whence arose the policy, which still continues in Indostan, of obliging the son to practice the profession of his father. After the discovery of letters, the facts of Astronomy and Chemistry became recorded in written language, though the antient hieroglyphic characters for the planets and metals continue in use at this day. The antiquity of the invention of music, of astronomical observations, and the manufacture of Gold and Iron, are recorded in Scripture.]

—The storied pyramid, the laurel'd bust,
The trophy'd arch had crumbled into dust;
The sacred symbol, and the epic song,
110 (Unknown the character, forgot the tongue,)
With each unconquer'd chief, or sainted maid,
Sunk undistinguish'd in Oblivion's shade.
Sad o'er the scatter'd ruins Genius sigh'd,
And infant Arts but learn'd to lisp and died.
115 Till to astonish'd realms PAPYRA taught
To paint in mystic colours Sound and Thought.
With Wisdom's voice to print the page sublime,
And mark in adamant the steps of Time.
—Three favour'd youths her soft attention share,
120 The fond disciples of the studious Fair,

Paper & progress for language [handwritten annotation]

[About twenty letters, ten cyphers, and seven crotches, represent by their numerous combinations all our ideas and sensations! the musical characters are probably arrived at their perfection, unless emphasis, and tone, and swell could be expressed, as well as note and time. Charles the Twelfth of Sweden had a design to have introduced a numeration by squares, instead of by decimation, which might have served the purposes of philosophy better than the present mode, which is said to be of Arabic invention. The alphabet is yet in a very imperfect state; perhaps seventeen letters could express all the simple sounds in the European languages. In China they have not yet learned to divide their words into syllables, and are thence necessitated to employ many thousand characters; it is said above eighty thousand. It is to be wished, in this ingenious age, that the European nations would accord to reform our alphabet.]

Hear her sweet voice, the golden process prove;
Gaze, as they learn; and, as they listen, love.
The first from Alpha to Omega joins
The letter'd tribes along the level lines;
125 Weighs with nice ear the vowel, liquid, surd,
And breaks in syllables the volant word.
Then forms *the next* upon the marshal'd plain
In deepening ranks his dexterous cypher-train;
And counts, as wheel the decimating bands,

130   The dews of Ægypt, or Arabia's sands,
      And then *the third* on four concordant lines
      Prints the lone crotchet, and the quaver joins;
      Marks the gay trill, the solemn pause inscribes,
      And parts with bars the undulating tribes.
135   Pleased round her cane-wove throne, the applauding crowd
      Clap'd their rude hands, their swarthy foreheads bow'd;
      With loud acclaim "a present God!" they cry'd,
      "A present God!" rebellowing shores reply'd—
      Then peal'd at intervals with mingled swell
140   The echoing harp, shrill clarion, horn, and shell;
      While Bards ecstatic, bending o'er the lyre,
      Struck deeper chords, and wing'd the song with fire.
      Then mark'd Astronomers with keener eyes
      The Moon's refulgent journey through the skies;
145   Watch'd the swift Comets urge their blazing cars,
      And weigh'd the Sun with his revolving Stars.
      High raised the Chemists their Hermetic wands,
      (And changing forms obey'd their waving hands,)
      Her treasur'd gold from Earth's deep chambers tore,
150   Or fused and harden'd her chalybeate ore.
      All with bent knee from fair PAPYRA claim
      Wove by her hands the wreath of deathless fame.
      —Exulting Genius crown'd his darling child,
      The young Arts clasp'd her knees, and Virtue smiled.
155   So now DELANY forms her mimic bowers,
      Her paper foliage, and her silken flowers;

[*So now Delany.* l. 155. Mrs. Delany has finished nine hundred and seventy accurate and elegant representations of different vegetables with the parts of their flowers, fructification, &c. according with the classification of Linneus, in what she terms paper-mosaic. She began this work at the age of 74, when her sight would no longer serve her to paint, in which she much excelled; between her age of 74 and 82, at which time her eyes quite failed her, she executed the curious Hortus ficcus above-mentioned, which I suppose contains a greater number of plants than were ever before drawn from the life by any one person. Her method consisted in placing the leaves of each plant with the petals, and all the other parts of the flowers, on coloured paper, and cutting them with scissars accurately to the natural size and form, and then parting them on a dark ground; the effect of which is wonderful, and their accuracy less liable to fallacy than drawings. She is at this time (1788) in her 89th year, with all the powers of a fine understanding still unimpaired. I am informed another very ingenious lady, Mrs. North, is constructing a similar Hortus ficcus, or Paper-garden; which she executes on a ground of vellum with such elegant taste and scientific accuracy, that it cannot fail to become a work of inestimable value.]

Her virgin train the tender scissars ply,
Vein the green leaf, the purple petal dye:
Round wiry stems the flaxen tendril bends,
160 Moss creeps below, and waxen fruit impends.
Cold Winter views amid his realms of snow
DELANY'S vegetable statues blow;
Smooths his stern brow, delays his hoary wing,
And eyes with wonder all the blooms of spring.

165 The gentle LAPSANA, NYMPHÆA fair,
And bright CALENDULA with golden hair,

many
medical
uses

watch of
Flora

[*Lapsana, Nymphæa alba, Calendula.* l. 165. And many other flowers close and open their petals at certain hours of the day; and thus constitute what Linneus calls the Horologe, or Watch of Flora. He enumerates 46 flowers, which possess this kind of sensibility. I shall mention a few of them with their respective hours of rising and setting, as Linneus terms them. He divides them first into *meteoric* flowers, which less accurately observe the hour of unfolding, but are expanded sooner or later, according to the cloudiness, moisture, or pressure of the atmosphere. 2d. *Tropical* flowers open in the morning and close before evening every day; but the hour of the expanding becomes earlier or later, at the length of the day increases or decreases. 3dly. *Æquinoctial* flowers, which open at a certain and exact hour of the day, and for the most part close at another determinate hour.

Hence the Horologe or Watch of Flora is formed from numerous plants, of which the following are those most common in this country. Leontodon taraxacum, Dandelion, opens at 5—6, closes at 8—9. Hieracium pilosella, mouse-ear hawkweed, opens at 8, closes at 2. Sonchus lævis, smooth Sow-thistle, at 5 and at 11—12. Lactuca sativa, cultivated Lettice, at 7 and jo. Tragopogon luteum, yellow Goatsbeard, at 3—5 and at 9—10. Lapsana, nipplewort, at 5—6 and at 10—1. Nymphæa alba, white water lily, at 7 and 5. Papaver nudicaule, naked poppy, at 5 and at 7. Hemerecallis fulva, tawny Day-lily, at 5 and at 7—8. Convolvulus, at 5—6. Malva, Mallow, at 9—10, and at 1. Arenarea purpurea, purple Sandwort, at 9—10, and at 2—3. Anagallis, pimpernel, at 7—8. Portulaca hortensis, garden Purilain, at 9—10, and at 11—12. Dianthus prolifer, proliferous Pink, at 8 and at 1. Cichoreum, Succory, at 4—5. Hypochiaeris, at 6—7, and at 4—5. Crepis at 4—5, and at 10—II. Picris, at 4—5, and at 12. Calendula field, at 9, and at 3. Calendula African, at 7, and at 3—4.

As these observations were probably made in the botanic gardens at Upsal, they must require further attention to suit them to our climate. See Stillingfleet Calendar of Flora.]

Watch with nice eye the Earth's diurnal way,
Marking her solar and sidereal day,
Her slow nutation, and her varying clime,
170 And trace with mimic art the march of Time;
Round his light foot a magic chain they fling,
And count the quick vibrations of his wing.—
First in its brazen cell reluctant roll'd
Bends the dark spring in many a steely fold;
175 On spiral brass is stretch'd the wiry thong,
Tooth urges tooth, and wheel drives wheel along;
In diamond-eyes the polish'd axles flow,
Smooth slides the hand, the ballance pants below.
Round the white circlet in relievo bold
180 A Serpent twines his scaly length in gold;
And brightly pencil'd on the enamel'd sphere
Live the fair trophies of the passing year.
—Here *Time's* huge fingers grasp his giant-mace,
And dash proud Superstition from her base,
185 Rend her strong towers and gorgeous fanes, and shed
The crumbling fragments round her guilty head.
There the gay *Hours*, whom wreaths of roses deck,
Lead their young trains amid the cumberous wreck;
And, slowly purpling o'er the mighty waste,
190 Plant the fair growths of Science and of Taste.
While each light *Moment*, as it dances by
With feathery foot and pleasure-twinkling eye,
Feeds from its baby-hand, with many a kiss,
The callow nestlings of domestic Bliss.

195 As yon gay clouds, which canopy the skies,
Change their thin forms, and lose their lucid dyes;
So the soft bloom of Beauty's vernal charms
Fades in our eyes, and withers in our arms.
—Bright as the silvery plume, or pearly shell,
200 The snow-white rose, or lily's virgin bell,
The fair HELLEBORAS attractive shone,
Warm'd every Sage, and every Shepherd won.—
Round the gay sisters press the *enamour'd bands*,
And seek with soft solicitude their hands.
205 —Ere while how chang'd!—in dim suffusion lies
The glance divine, that lighten'd in their eyes;

[*Helleborus.* I. 201. Many males, many females. The Helleborus niger, or Christmas rose, has a large beautiful white flower, adorned with a circle of tubular two-lipp'd nectaries. After impregnation the flower undergoes a remarkable change, the nectaries drop off, but the white corol remains, and gradually becomes quite green. This curious metamorphose of the corol, when the nectaries fall off, seems to shew that the white juices of the corol were before carried to the nectaries, for the purpose of producing honey: because when these nectaries fall off, no more of the white juice is secreted in the corol, but it becomes green, and degenerates into a calyx. See note on Lonicera. The nectary of the Tropaeolum, garden nasturtion, is a coloured horn growing from the calyx.]

Cold are those lips, where smiles seductive hung,
And the weak accents linger on their tongue;
Each roseat feature fades to livid green,—
210   —Disgust with face averted shuts the scene.

So from his gorgeous throne, which awed the world,
The mighty Monarch of the east was hurl'd,
To dwell with brutes beneath the midnight storm,
By Heaven's just vengeance changed in mind and form.
215   —Prone to the earth He bends his brow superb,
Crops the young floret and the bladed herb;
Lolls his red tongue, and from the reedy side
Of slow Euphrates laps the muddy tide.
Long eagle-plumes his arching neck invest,
220 Steal round his arms, and clasp his sharpen'd breast;
Dark brinded hairs in bristling ranks, behind,
Rise o'er his back, and rustle in the wind,
Clothe his lank sides, his shrivel'd limbs surround,
And human hands with talons print the ground.
225 Silent in shining troops the Courtier-throng
Pursue their monarch as he crawls along;
E'en Beauty pleads in vain with smiles and tears,
Nor Flattery's self can pierce his pendant ears.

Two Sister-Nymphs to Ganges' flowery brink
230 Bend their light steps, the lucid water drink,
Wind through the dewy rice, and nodding canes,
(As *eight* black Eunuchs guard the sacred plains),
With playful malice watch the scaly brood,
And shower the inebriate berries on the flood.—
235 Stay in your crystal chambers, silver tribes!
Turn your bright eyes, and shun the dangerous bribes;
The tramel'd net with less destruction sweeps
Your curling shallows, and your azure deeps;
With less deceit, the gilded fly beneath,
240 Lurks the fell hook unseen,—to taste is death!—

—Dim your slow eyes, and dull your pearly coat,
Drunk on the waves your languid forms shall float,

[*Two Sister-Nymphs.* l. 229. Menispernum. Cocculus. Indian berry. Two
houses, twelve males. In the female flower there are two styles and eight
filaments without anthers on their summits; which are called by Linneus
eunuchs. See the note on Curcuma. The berry intoxicates fish. Saint Anthony of
Padua, when the people refused to hear him, preached to the fish, and converted
them. Addison's travels in Italy.]

On useless fins in giddy circles play,
And Herons and Otters seize you for their prey.—

245 So, when the Saint from Padua's graceless land
In silent anguish sought the barren strand,
High on the shatter'd beech sublime He stood,
Still'd with his waving arm the babbling flood;
"To Man's dull ear," He cry'd, "I call in vain,
"Hear me, ye scaly tenants of the main!"—
250 Misshapen Seals approach in circling flocks,
In dusky mail the Tortoise climbs the rocks,
Torpedoes, Sharks, Rays, Porpus, Dolphins, pour
Their twinkling squadrons round the glittering shore;
255 With tangled fins, behind, huge Phocæ glide,
And Whales and Grampi swell the distant tide.
Then kneel'd the hoary Seer, to heaven address'd
His fiery eyes, and smote his sounding breast;
"Bless ye the Lord!" with thundering voice he cry'd,
260 "Bless ye the Lord!" the bending shores reply'd;
The winds and waters caught the sacred word,
And mingling echoes shouted "Bless the Lord!"
The listening shoals the quick contagion feel,
Pant on the floods, inebriate with their zeal,
265 Ope their wide jaws, and bow their slimy heads,
And dash with frantic fins their foamy beds.

Sopha'd on silk, amid her charm-built towers,
Her meads of asphodel, and amaranth bowers,
Where Sleep and Silence guard the soft abodes,
270 In sullen apathy PAPAVER nods.
Faint o'er her couch in scintillating streams
Pass the thin forms of Fancy and of Dreams;
Froze by inchantment on the velvet ground
Fair youths and beauteous ladies glitter round;

[*Papaver.* l. 270. Poppy. Many males, many females. The plants of this class are almost all of them poisonous; the finest opium is procured by wounding the heads of large poppies with a three-edged knife, and tying muscle-shells to them to catch the drops. In small quantities it exhilarates the mind, raises the passions, and invigorates the body: in large ones it is succeeded by intoxication, languor, stupor and death. It is customary in India for a messenger to travel above a hundred miles without rest or food, except an appropriated bit of opium for himself, and a larger one for his horse at certain stages. The emaciated and decrepid appearance, with the ridiculous and idiotic gestures, of the opium-eaters in Constantinople is well described in the Memoirs of Baron de Tott.]

275 On crystal pedestals they seem to sigh,
    Bend the meek knee, and lift the imploring eye.
    —And now the Sorceress bares her shrivel'd hand,
    And circles thrice in air her ebon wand;
    Flush'd with new life descending statues talk,
280 The pliant marble softening as they walk;
    With deeper sobs reviving lovers breathe,
    Fair bosoms rise, and soft hearts pant beneath;
    With warmer lips relenting damsels speak,
    And kindling blushes tinge the Parian cheek;
285 To viewless lutes aërial voices sing,
    And hovering Loves are heard on rustling wing.
    —She waves her wand again!—fresh horrors seize
    Their stiffening limbs, their vital currents freeze;
    By each cold nymph her marble lover lies,
290 And iron slumbers seal their glassy eyes.
    So with his dread Caduceus HERMES led
    From the dark regions of the imprison'd dead,
    Or drove in silent shoals the lingering train
    To Night's dull shore, and PLUTO'S dreary reign
295 So with her waving pencil CREWE commands
    The realms of Taste, and Fancy's fairy lands;
    Calls up with magic voice the shapes, that sleep
    In earth's dark bosom, or unfathom'd deep;
    That shrined in air on viewless wings aspire,
300 Or blazing bathe in elemental fire.
    As with nice touch her plastic hand she moves,
    Rise the fine forms of Beauties, Graces, Loves;
    Kneel to the fair Inchantress, smile or sigh,
    And fade or flourish, as she turns her eye.

305 Fair CISTA, rival of the rosy dawn,
    Call'd her light choir, and trod the dewy lawn;
    Hail'd with rude melody the new-born May,

As cradled yet in April's lap she lay.

[*So with her waving pencil.* l. 295. Alluding to the many beautiful paintings by Miss EMMA CREWE; to whom the author is indebted for the very elegant Frontispiece, where Flora, at play with Cupid, is loading him with garden-tools.]

[*Cistus labdaniferus.* l. 304. Many males, one female. The petals of this beautiful and fragrant shrub, as well as of the Oenothera, tree primrose, and others, continue expanded but a few hours, falling off about noon, or soon after, in hot weather. The most beautiful flowers of the Cactus grandiflorus (see Cerea) are of equally short duration, but have their existence in the night. And the flowers of the Hibiscus trionum are said to continue but a single hour. The courtship between the males and females in these flowers might be easily watched; the males are said to approach and recede from the females alternately. The flowers of the Hibiscus sinensis, mutable rose, live in the West Indies, their native climate, but one day; but have this remarkable property, they are white at the first expansion, then change to deep red, and become purple as they decay.

The gum or resin of this fragrant vegetable is collected from extensive underwoods of it in the East by a singular contrivance. Long leathern thongs are tied to poles and cords, and drawn over the tops of these shrubs about noon; which thus collect the dust of the anthers, which adheres to the leather, and is occasionally scraped off. Thus in some degree is the manner imitated, in which the bee collects on his thighs and legs the same material for the construction of his combs.]

I.

"Born in yon blaze of orient sky,
310   "Sweet MAY! thy radiant form unfold;
    "Unclose thy blue voluptuous eye,
    "And wave thy shadowy locks of gold.

II.

"For Thee the fragrant zephyrs blow,
    "For Thee descends the sunny shower;
315   "The rills in softer murmurs flow,
    "And brighter blossoms gem the bower.

III.

"Light Graces dress'd in flowery wreaths
    "And tiptoe Joys their hands combine;
    "And Love his sweet contagion breathes,
320   "And laughing dances round thy shrine.

IV.

"Warm with new life the glittering throngs
"On quivering fin and rustling wing
"Delighted join their votive songs,
"And hail thee, GODDESS OF THE SPRING."

325 O'er the green brinks of Severn's oozy bed,
   In changeful rings, her sprightly troop She led;
   PAN tripp'd before, where Eudness shades the mead,
   And blew with glowing lip his sevenfold reed;
   Emerging Naiads swell'd the jocund strain,
330 And aped with mimic step the dancing train.—

[*Sevenfold reed.* I. 328. The sevenfold reed, with which Pan is frequently described, seems to indicate, that he was the inventor of the musical gamut.]

"I faint, I fall!"—*at noon* the Beauty cried,
   "Weep o'er my tomb, ye Nymphs!"—and sunk and died.
   —Thus, when white Winter o'er the shivering clime
   Drives the still snow, or showers the silver rime;
335 As the lone shepherd o'er the dazzling rocks
   Prints his steep step, and guides his vagrant flocks;
   Views the green holly veil'd in network nice,
   Her vermil clusters twinkling in the ice;
   Admires the lucid vales, and slumbering floods,
340 Fantastic cataracts, and crystal woods,
   Transparent towns, with seas of milk between,
   And eyes with transport the refulgent scene:—
   If breaks the sunshine o'er the spangled trees,
   Or flits on tepid wing the western breeze,
345 In liquid dews descends the transient glare,
   And all the glittering pageant melts in air.
   Where Andes hides his cloud-wreath'd crest in snow,
   And roots his base on burning sands below;
   Cinchona, fairest of Peruvian maids
350 To Health's bright Goddess in the breezy glades
   On Quito's temperate plain an altar rear'd,
   Trill'd the loud hymn, the solemn prayer preferr'd:
   Each balmy bud she cull'd, and honey'd flower,
   And hung with fragrant wreaths the sacred bower;
355 Each pearly sea she search'd, and sparkling mine,
   And piled their treasures on the gorgeous shrine;
   Her suppliant voice for sickening Loxa raised,
   Sweet breath'd the gale, and bright the censor blazed.

—"Divine HYGEIA! on thy votaries bend
360 Thy angel-looks, oh, hear us, and defend!
    While streaming o'er the night with baleful glare
    The star of Autumn rays his misty hair;
    Fierce from his fens the Giant AGUE springs,
    And wrapp'd in fogs descends on vampire wings;

[*Cinchona.* l. 349. Peruvian bark-tree. Five males, and one female. Several of these trees were felled for other purposes into a lake, when an epidemic fever of a very mortal kind prevailed at Loxa in Peru, and the woodmen, accidentally drinking the water, were cured; and thus were discovered the virtues of this famous drug.]

365 "Before, with shuddering limbs cold Tremor reels,
    And Fever's burning nostril dogs his heels;
    Loud claps the grinning Fiend his iron hands,
    Stamps with his marble feet, and shouts along the lands;
    Withers the damask cheek, unnerves the strong,
370 And drives with scorpion-lash the shrieking throng.
    Oh, Goddess! on thy kneeling votaries bend
    Thy angel-looks, oh, hear us, and defend!"
    —HYGEIA, leaning from the blest abodes,
    The crystal mansions of the immortal gods,
375 Saw the sad Nymph uplift her dewy eyes,
    Spread her white arms, and breathe her fervid sighs;
    Call'd to her fair associates, Youth, and Joy,
    And shot all-radiant through the glittering sky;
    Loose waved behind her golden train of hair,
380 Her sapphire mantle swam diffus'd in air.—
    O'er the grey matted moss, and pansied sod,
    With step sublime the glowing Goddess trod,
    Gilt with her beamy eye the conscious shade,
    And with her smile celestial bless'd the maid.
385 "Come to my arms," with seraph voice she cries,
    "Thy vows are heard, benignant Nymph! arise;
    Where yon aspiring trunks fantastic wreath
    Their mingled roots, and drink the rill beneath,
    Yield to the biting axe thy sacred wood,
390 And strew the bitter foliage on the flood."
    In silent homage bow'd the blushing maid,—
    Five youths athletic hasten to her aid,
    O'er the scar'd hills re-echoing strokes resound,
    And headlong forests thunder on the ground.
395 Round the dark roots, rent bark, and shatter'd boughs,

From ocherous beds the swelling fountain flows;
With streams austere its winding margin laves,
And pours from vale to vale its dusky waves.
—As the pale squadrons, bending o'er the brink,
400 View with a sigh their alter'd forms, and drink;
Slow-ebbing life with refluent crimson breaks
O'er their wan lips, and paints their haggard cheeks;
Through each fine nerve rekindling transports dart,
Light the quick eye, and swell the exulting heart.
405 —Thus ISRAEL's heaven-taught chief o'er trackless lands
Led to the sultry rock his murmuring bands.
Bright o'er his brows the forky radiance blazed,
And high in air the rod divine He raised.—
Wide yawns the cliff!—amid the thirsty throng
410 Rush the redundant waves, and shine along;
With gourds and shells and helmets press the bands,
Ope their parch'd lips, and spread their eager hands,
Snatch their pale infants to the exuberant shower,
Kneel on the shatter'd rock, and bless the Almighty Power.

415 Bolster'd with down, amid a thousand wants,
Pale Dropsy rears his bloated form, and pants;
"Quench me, ye cool pellucid rills!" he cries,
Wets his parch'd tongue, and rolls his hollow eyes.
So bends tormented TANTALUS to drink,
420 While from his lips the refluent waters shrink;
Again the rising stream his bosom laves,
And Thirst consumes him 'mid circumfluent waves.
—Divine HYGEIA, from the bending sky
Descending, listens to his piercing cry;
425 Assumes bright DIGITALIS' dress and air,
Her ruby cheek, white neck, and raven hair;
Four youths protect her from the circling throng,
And like the Nymph the Goddess steps along.—
—O'er Him She waves her serpent-wreathed wand,
430 Cheers with her voice, and raises with her hand,
Warms with rekindling bloom his visage wan,
And charms the shapeless monster into man.

[*Digitalis.* l. 425. Of the class Two Powers. Four males, one female, Foxglove. The effect of this plant in that kind of Dropsy, which is termed anasarca, where the legs and thighs are much swelled, attended with great difficulty of breathing, is truly astonishing. In the ascites accompanied with anasarca of people past the meridian of life it will also sometimes succeed. The method of administering it requires some caution, as it is liable, in greater doses, to induce very violent and debilitating sickness, which continues on days, during which time the dropsical collection however disappears. (spoonful, or half an ounce, of the following decoction, given twice a generally succeed in a few days. But in more robust people, one large spoonful every two hours, till four spoonfuls are taken, or till sickness occurs, will evacuate the dropsical swellings with greater certainty, but is liable to operate more violently. Boil four ounces of the fresh leaves of purple Foxglove (which leaves may be had at all seasons of the year) from two pints of water to twelve ounces; add to the strained liquor, while yet warm, three ounces of rectified spirit of wine. A theory of the effects of this medicine, with many successful cases, may be seen in a pamphlet, called, "Experiments on Mucilaginous and Purulent Matter," published by Dr. Darwin in 1780. Sold by Cadell, London.]

So when Contagion with mephitic breath
And withered Famine urged the work of death;
435   Marseilles' good Bishop, London's generous Mayor,
With food and faith, with medicine and with prayer,
Raised the weak head and stayed the parting sigh,
Or with new life relumed the swimming eye.—
440   —And now, PHILANTHROPY! thy rays divine
Dart round the globe from Zembla to the Line;
O'er each dark prison plays the cheering light,
Like northern lustres o'er the vault of night.—

[*Marseillle's good Bishop*. l. 435. In the year 1720 and 1722 the Plague made dreadful havock at Marseilles; at which time the Bishop was indefatigable in the execution of his pastoral office, visiting, relieving, encouraging, and absolving the sick with extream tenderness; and though perpetually exposed to the infection, like Sir John Lawrence mentioned below, they both are said to have escaped the disease.]

[*London's generous Mayor*, l. 435. During the great Plague at London in the year 1665, Sir John Lawrence, the then Lord Mayor, continued the whole time in the city; heard complaints, and redressed them; enforced the wisest regulations then known, and saw them executed. The day after the disease was known with certainty to be the Plague, above 40,000 servants were dismissed, and turned into the streets to perish, for no one would receive them into their houses; and the villages near London drove them away with pitch-forks and fire-arms. Sir John Lawrence supported them all, as well as the needy who were sick, at first by expending his own fortune, till subscriptions could be solicited and received from all parts of the nation. *Journal of the Plague-year, Printed for E. Nutt, &c. at the R. Exchange. 1722.*]

From realm to realm, with cross or crescent crown'd,
Where'er Mankind and Misery are found,
445   O'er burning sands, deep waves, or wilds of snow,

Thy HOWARD journeying seeks the house of woe.
Down many a winding step to dungeons dank,
Where anguish wails aloud, and fetters clank;
To caves bestrew'd with many a mouldering bone,
450 And cells, whose echoes only learn to groan;
Where no kind bars a whispering friend disclose,
No sunbeam enters, and no zephyr blows,
HE treads, inemulous of fame or wealth,
Profuse of toil, and prodigal of health;
455 With soft assuasive eloquence expands
Power's rigid heart, and opes his clenching hands;
Leads stern-ey'd Justice to the dark domains,
If not to sever, to relax the chains;
Or guides awaken'd Mercy through the gloom,
460 And shews the prison, sister to the tomb!—
Gives to her babes the self-devoted wife,
To her fond husband liberty and life!—
—The Spirits of the Good, who bend from high
Wide o'er these earthly scenes their partial eye,
465 When first, array'd in VIRTUE'S purest robe,
They saw her HOWARD traversing the globe;
Saw round his brows her sun-like Glory blaze
In arrowy circles of unwearied rays;
Mistook a Mortal for an Angel-Guest,
470 And ask'd what Seraph-foot the earth imprest.
—Onward he moves!—Disease and Death retire,
And murmuring Demons hate him, and admire."

Here paused the Goddess,—on HYGEIA'S shrine
Obsequious Gnomes repose the lyre divine;
475 Descending Sylphs relax the trembling strings,
And catch the rain-drops on their shadowy wings.
—And now her vase a modest Naiad fills
With liquid crystal from her pebbly rills;
Piles the dry cedar round her silver urn,
480 (Bright climbs the blaze, the crackling faggots burn),
Culls the green herb of China's envy'd bowers,
In gaudy cups the steamy treasure pours;
And, sweetly-smiling, on her bended knee
Presents the fragrant quintessence of Tea.

INTERLUDE II.

Bookseller. The monsters of your Botanic Garden are as surprising as the bulls with brazen feet, and the fire-breathing dragons, which guarded the Hesperian fruit; yet are they not disgusting, nor mischievous: and in the manner you have chained them together in your exhibition, they succeed each other amusingly enough, like prints of the London Cries, wrapped upon rollers, with a glass before them. In this at least they resemble the monsters in <u>Ovid's Metamorphoses</u>; but your similies, I suppose, are Homeric?

Poet. The great Bard well understood how to make use of this kind of ornament in Epic Poetry. He brings his valiant heroes into the field with much parade, and sets them a fighting with great fury; and then, after a few thrusts and parries, he introduces a long string of similies. During this the battle is supposed to continue; and thus the time necessary for the action is gained in our imaginations; and a degree of probability produced, which contributes to the temporary deception or reverie of the reader.

But the similies of Homer have another agreeable characteristic; they do not quadrate, or go upon all fours (as it is called), like the more formal similies of some modern writers; any one resembling feature seems to be with him a sufficient excuse for the introduction of this kind of digression; he then proceeds to deliver some agreeable poetry on this new subject, and thus converts every simile into a kind of short episode.

B. Then a simile should not very accurately resemble the subject?

P. No; it would then become a philosophical analogy, it would be ratiocination instead of poetry: it need only so far resemble the subject, as poetry itself ought to resemble nature. It should have so much sublimity, beauty, or novelty, as to interest the reader; and should be expressed in picturesque language, so as to bring the scenery before his eye; and should lastly bear so much veri-similitude as not to awaken him by the violence of improbability or incongruity.

B. May not the reverie of the reader be dissipated or disturbed by disagreeable images being presented to his imagination, as well as by improbable or incongruous ones?

P. Certainly; he will endeavour to rouse himself from a disagreeable reverie, as from the night-mare. And from this may be discovered the line of boundary between the Tragic and the Horrid: which line, however, will veer a little this way or that, according to the prevailing manners of the age or country, and the peculiar associations of ideas, or idiosyncracy of mind, of individuals. For instance, if an artist should represent the death of an officer in battle, by shewing a little blood on the bosom of his shirt, as if a bullet had there penetrated, the dying figure would affect the beholder with pity; and if fortitude was at the same time expressed in his countenance, admiration would be added to our pity. On the contrary, if the artist should chuse to represent his thigh as shot away by a cannon ball, and should exhibit the bleeding flesh and shattered bone of the stump, the picture would introduce into our minds ideas from a butcher's shop, or a surgeon's operation-room, and we should turn from it with disgust. So if characters were brought upon the stage with their limbs disjointed by torturing instruments, and the floor covered with clotted blood and scattered brains, our theatric reverie would be destroyed by disgust, and we should leave the play-house with detestation.

The Painters have been more guilty in this respect than the Poets; the cruelty of Apollo in flaying Marcias alive is a favourite subject with the antient artists: and the tortures of expiring martyrs have disgraced the modern ones. It requires little genius to exhibit the muscles in convulsive action either by the pencil or the chissel, because the interstices are deep, and the lines strongly defined: but those tender gradations of muscular action, which constitute the graceful attitudes of the body, are difficult to conceive or to execute, except by a master of nice discernment and cultivated taste.

B. By what definition would you distinguish the Horrid from the Tragic?

P. I suppose the latter consists of Distress attended with Pity, which is said to be allied to Love, the most agreeable of all our passions; and the former in Distress, accompanied with Disgust, which is allied to Hate, and is one of our most disagreeable sensations. Hence, when horrid scenes of cruelty are represented in pictures, we wish to disbelieve their existence, and voluntarily exert ourselves to escape from the deception: whereas the bitter cup of true Tragedy is mingled with some sweet consolatory drops, which endear our tears, and we continue to contemplate the interesting delusion with a delight which it is not easy to explain.

B. Has not this been explained by Lucretius, where he describes a shipwreck; and says, the Spectators receive pleasure from feeling themselves safe on land? and by Akenside, in his beautiful poem on the Pleasures of Imagination, who ascribes it to our finding objects for the due exertion of our passions?

P. We must not confound our sensations at the contemplation of real misery with those which we experience at the scenical representations of tragedy. The spectators of a shipwreck may be attracted by the dignity and novelty of the object; and from these may be said to receive pleasure; but not from the distress of the sufferers. An ingenious writer, who has criticised this dialogue in the English Review for August, 1789, adds, that one great source of our pleasure from scenical distress arises from our, at the same time, generally contemplating one of the noblest objects of nature, that of Virtue triumphant over every difficulty and oppression, or supporting its votary under every suffering: or, where this does not occur, that our minds are relieved by the justice of some signal punishment awaiting the delinquent. But, besides this, at the exhibition of a good tragedy, we are not only amused by the dignity, and novelty, and beauty, of the objects before us; but, if any distressful circumstances occur too forcible for our sensibility, we can voluntarily exert ourselves, and recollect, that the scenery is not real: and thus not only the pain, which we had received from the apparent distress, is lessened, but a new source of pleasure is opened to us, similar to that which we frequently have felt on awaking from a distressful dream; we are glad that it is not true. We are at the same time unwilling to relinquish the pleasure which we receive from the other interesting circumstances of the drama; and on that account quickly permit ourselves to relapse into the delusion; and thus alternately believe and disbelieve, almost every moment, the existence of the objects represented before us.

B. Have those two sovereigns of poetic land, HOMER and SHAKESPEAR, kept their works entirely free from the Horrid?—or even yourself in your third Canto?

P. The descriptions of the mangled carcasses of the companions of Ulysses, in the cave of Polypheme, is in this respect certainly objectionable, as is well observed by Scaliger. And in the play of Titus Andronicus, if that was written by Shakespear (which from its internal evidence I think very improbable), there are many horrid and disgustful circumstances. The following Canto is submitted to the candour of the critical reader, to whose opinion I shall submit in silence.

Frankness; Honesty

THE LOVES OF THE PLANTS.

CANTO III.

And now the Goddess sounds her silver shell,
And shakes with deeper tones the inchanted dell;
Pale, round her grassy throne, bedew'd with tears,
Flit the thin forms of Sorrows, and of Fears;
5   Soft Sighs responsive whisper to the chords,
And Indignations half-unsheath their swords.
"Thrice round the grave CIRCÆA prints her tread,
And chaunts the numbers, which disturb the dead;
Shakes o'er the holy earth her sable plume,
10   Waves her dread wand, and strikes the echoing tomb!
—Pale shoot the stars across the troubled night,
The timorous moon withholds her conscious light;
Shrill scream the famish'd bats, and shivering owls,
And loud and long the dog of midnight howls!—

[*Circæa*. l. 7. Enchanter's Nightshade. Two males, one female. It was much celebrated in the mysteries of witchcraft, and for the purpose of raising the devil, as its name imports. It grows amid the mouldering bones and decayed coffins in the ruinous vaults of Sleaford-church in Lincolnshire. The superstitious ceremonies or histories belonging to some vegetables have been truly ridiculous; thus the Druids are said to have cropped the Misletoe with a golden axe or sickle; and the Bryony, or Mandrake, was said to utter a scream when its root was drawn from the ground; and that the animal which drew it up became diseased and soon died: on which account, when it was wanted for the purposes of medicine, it was usual to loosen and remove the earth about the root, and then to tie it by means of a cord to a dog's tail, who was whipped to pull it up, and was then supposed to suffer for the impiety of the action. And even at this day bits of dried root of Peony are rubbed smooth, and strung, and sold under the name of Anodyne necklaces, and tied round the necks of children, to facilitate the growth of their teeth! add to this, that in Price's History of Cornwall, a book published about ten years ago, the Virga Divinatoria, or Divining Rod, has a degree of credit given to it. This rod is of hazle, or other light wood, and held horizontally in the hand, and is said to bow towards the ore whenever the Conjurer walks over a mine. A very few years ago, in France, and even in England, another kind of divining rod has been used to discover springs of water in a similar manner, and gained some credit. And in the very last year, there were many in France, and some in England, who underwent an enchantment without any divining rod at all, and believed themselves to be affected by an invisible agent, which the Enchanter called Animal Magnetism!]

—Then yawns the bursting ground!—*two* imps obscene

Rise on broad wings, and hail the baleful queen;
Each with dire grin salutes the potent wand,
And leads the sorceress with his sooty hand;
Onward they glide, where sheds the sickly yew
20   O'er many a mouldering bone its nightly dew;
The ponderous portals of the church unbar,—
Hoarse on their hinge the ponderous portals jar;
As through the colour'd glass the moon-beam falls,
Huge shapeless spectres quiver on the walls;
25   Low murmurs creep along the hollow ground,
And to each step the pealing ailes resound;
By glimmering lamps, protecting saints among,
The shrines all tremble as they pass along,
O'er the still choir with hideous laugh they move,
30   (Fiends yell below, and angels weep above!)
Their impious march to God's high altar bend,
With feet impure the sacred steps ascend;
With wine unbless'd the holy chalice stain,
Assume the mitre, and the cope profane;
35   To heaven their eyes in mock devotion throw,
And to the cross with horrid mummery bow;
Adjure by mimic rites the powers above,
And plight alternate their Satanic love.

Avaunt, ye Vulgar! from her sacred groves
40   With maniac step the Pythian LAURA moves;
Full of the God her labouring bosom sighs,
Foam on her lips, and fury in her eyes,
Strong writhe her limbs, her wild dishevell'd hair
Starts from her laurel-wreath, and swims in air.—
45   While *twenty* Priests the gorgeous shrine surround
Cinctur'd with ephods, and with garlands crown'd,

[*Laura.* l. 40. Prunus. Lauro-cerasus. Twenty males, one female. The Pythian priestess is supposed to have been made drunk with infusion of laurel-leaves when she delivered her oracles. The intoxication or inspiration is finely described by Virgil. Æn. L. vi. The distilled water from laurel-leaves is, perhaps, the most sudden poison we are acquainted with in this country. I have seen about two spoonfuls of it destroy a large pointer dog in less than ten minutes. In a smaller dose it is said to produce intoxication: on this account there is reason to believe it acts in the same manner as opium and vinous spirit; but that the dose is not so well ascertained. See note on Tremella. It is used in the Ratafie of the distillers, by which some dram-drinkers have been suddenly killed. One pint of water, distilled from fourteen pounds of black cherry stones bruised, has the same deleterious effect, destroying as suddenly as laurel-water. It is probable

ernels, Peach-leaves, Walnut-leaves, and whatever possesses the kernel-
ay have similar qualities.]

Contending hosts and trembling nations wait
The firm immutable behests of Fate;
—She speaks in thunder from her golden throne
50 With words *unwill'd*, and wisdom not her own.

So on his NIGHTMARE through the evening fog
Flits the squab Fiend o'er fen, and lake, and bog;
Seeks some love-wilder'd Maid with sleep oppress'd,
Alights, and grinning sits upon her breast.
55 —Such as of late amid the murky sky
Was mark'd by FUSELI'S poetic eye;
Whose daring tints, with SHAKESPEAR'S happiest grace,
Gave to the airy phantom form and place.—
Back o'er her pillow sinks her blushing head,
60 Her snow-white limbs hang helpless from the bed;
While with quick sighs, and suffocative breath,
Her interrupted heart-pulse swims in death.
—Then shrieks of captured towns, and widows' tears,
Pale lovers stretch'd upon their blood-stain'd biers,
65 The headlong precipice that thwarts her flight,
The trackless desert, the cold starless night,
And stern-eye'd Murder with his knife behind,
In dread succession agonize her mind.
O'er her fair limbs convulsive tremors fleet,
70 Start in her hands, and struggle in her feet;
In vain to scream with quivering lips she tries,
And strains in palsy'd lids her tremulous eyes;
In vain she *wills* to run, fly, swim, walk, creep;
The WILL presides not in the bower of SLEEP.
75 —On her fair bosom sits the Demon-Ape
Erect, and balances his bloated shape;

[*The Will presides not.* 1. 74. Sleep consists in the abolition of all voluntary
power, both over our muscular motions and our ideas; for we neither walk nor
reason in sleep. But, at the same time, many of our muscular motions, and many
of our ideas, continue to be excited into action in consequence of internal
irritations and of internal sensations; for the heart and arteries continue to beat,
and we experience variety of passions, and even hunger and thirst in our dreams.
Hence I conclude, that our nerves of sense are not torpid or inert during sleep;
but that they are only precluded from the perception of external objects, by their
external organs being rendered unfit to transmit to them the appulses of external
bodies, during the suspension of the power of volition; thus the eye-lids are

closed in sleep, and I suppose the tympanum of the ear is not stretched, because they are deprived of the voluntary exertions of the muscles appropriated to these purposes; and it is probable something similar happens to the external apparatus of our other organs of sense, which may render them unfit for their office of perception during sleep: for milk put into the mouths of sleeping babes occasions them to swallow and suck; and, if the eye-lid is a little opened in the day-light by the exertions of disturbed sleep, the person dreams of being much dazzled. See first Interlude.]

Rolls in their marble orbs his Gorgon-eyes,
And drinks with leathern ears her tender cries.

Arm'd with her ivory beak, and talon-hands,
80   Descending FICA dives into the sands;
Chamber'd in earth with cold oblivion lies;
Nor heeds, *ye Suitor-train*, your amorous sighs;
Erewhile with renovated beauty blooms,
Mounts into air, and moves her leafy plumes.
85   —Where HAMPS and MANIFOLD, their cliffs among,
Each in his flinty channel winds along;
With lucid lines the dusky Moor divides,
Hurrying to intermix their sister tides.

[When there arises in sleep a painful desire to exert the voluntary motions, it is called the Nightmare or Incubus. When the sleep becomes so imperfect that some muscular motions obey this exertion of desire, people have walked about, and even performed some domestic offices in sleep; one of these sleep-walkers I have frequently seen: once she smelt of a tube-rose, and sung, and drank a dish of tea in this state; her awaking was always attended with prodigious surprize, and even fear; this disease had daily periods, and seemed to be of the epileptic kind.]

[*Ficus indica.* l. 80. Indian Fig-tree. Of the glass Polygamy. This large tree rises with opposite branches on all sides, with long egged leaves; each branch emits a slender flexile depending appendage from its summit like a cord, which roots into the earth and rises again. Sloan. Hist. of Jamaica. Lin. Spec. Plant. See Capri-ficus.]

Where still their silver-bosom'd Nymphs abhor,
90   The blood-smear'd mansion of gigantic THOR,—
—Erst, fires volcanic in the marble womb
Of cloud-wrapp'd WETTON raised the massy dome;
Rocks rear'd on rocks in huge disjointed piles
Form the tall turrets, and the lengthen'd ailes;

[*Gigantic Thor.* l. 90. Near the village of Wetton, a mile or two above Dove-
Dale, near Ashburn in Dirbyshire, there is a spacious cavern about the middle of
the ascent of the mountain, which still retains the Name of Thor's house; below
is an extensive and romantic common, where the rivers Hamps and Manifold
sink into the earth, and rise again in Ham gardens, the seat of John Port, Esq.
about three miles below. Where these rivers rise again there are impressions
resembling Fish, which appear to be of Jasper bedded in Limestone. Calcareous
Spars, Shells converted into a kind of Agate, corallines in Marble, ores of Lead,
Copper, and Zinc, and many strata of Flint, or Chert, and of Toadstone, or
Lava, abound in this part of the country. The Druids are said to have offered
human sacrifices inclosed in wicker idols to Thor. Thursday had its name from
this Deity.

The broken appearance of the surface of many parts of this country; with
the Swallows, as they are called, or basons on some of the mountains, like
volcanic Craters, where the rain-water sinks into the earth; and the numerous
large stones, which seem to have been thrown over the land by volcanic
explosions; as well as the great masses of Toadstone or Lava; evince the
existence of violent earthquakes at some early period of the world. At this time
the channels of these subterraneous rivers seem to have been formed, when a
long tract of rocks were raised by the sea flowing in upon the central fires, and
thus producing an irresistable explosion of steam; and when these rocks again
subsided, their parts did not exactly correspond, but left a long cavity arched
over in this operation of nature. The cavities at Castleton and Buxton in
Derbyshire seem to have had a similar origin, as well as this cavern termed
Thor's house. See Mr. Whitehurst's and Dr. Hutton's Theories of the Earth.]

```
 95   Broad ponderous piers sustain the roof, and wide
        Branch the vast rain-bow ribs from side to side.
        While from above descends in milky streams
        One scanty pencil of illusive beams,
        Suspended crags and gaping gulphs illumes,
100   And gilds the horrors of the deepen'd glooms.
        —Here oft the Naiads, as they chanced to play
        Near the dread Fane on THOR'S returning day,
        Saw from red altars streams of guiltless blood
        Stain their green reed-beds, and pollute their flood;
105   Heard dying babes in wicker prisons wail,
        And shrieks of matrons thrill the affrighted Gale;
        While from dark caves infernal Echoes mock,
        And Fiends triumphant shout from every rock!
        —So still the Nymphs emerging lift in air
110   Their snow-white shoulders and their azure hair;
        Sail with sweet grace the dimpling streams along,
        Listening the Shepherd's or the Miner's song;
        But, when afar they view the giant-cave,
```

On timorous fins they circle on the wave,
115 With streaming eyes and throbbing hearts recoil,
Plunge their fair forms, and dive beneath the soil.—
Closed round their heads reluctant eddies sink,
And wider rings successive dash the brink.—
Three thousand steps in sparry clefts they stray,
120 Or seek through sullen mines their gloomy way;
On beds of Lava sleep in coral cells,
Or sigh o'er jasper fish, and agate shells.
Till, where famed ILAM leads his boiling floods
Through flowery meadows and impending woods,
125 Pleased with light spring they leave the dreary night,
And 'mid circumfluent surges rise to light;
Shake their bright locks, the widening vale pursue,
Their sea-green mantles fringed with pearly dew;
In playful groups by towering THORP they move,
130 Bound o'er the foaming wears, and rush into the Dove.

With fierce distracted eye IMPATIENS stands,
Swells her pale cheeks, and brandishes her hands,

[*Impatiens*. l. 131. Touch me not. The seed vessel consists of one cell with five divisions; each of these, when the seed is ripe, on being touched, suddenly folds itself into a spiral form, leaps from the stalk and disperses the seeds to a great distance by it's elasticity. The capsule of the geranium and the beard of wild oats are twisted for a similar purpose, and dislodge their seeds on wet days, when the ground is best fitted to receive them. Hence one of these, with its adhering capsule or beard fixed on a stand, serves the purpose of an hygrometer, twisting itself more or less according to the moisture of the air.

The awn of barley is furnished with stiff points, which, like the teeth of a saw, are all turned towards the point of it; as this long awn lies upon the ground, it extends itself in the moist air of night, and pushes forwards the barley corn, which it adheres to; in the day it shortens as it dries; and as these points prevent it from receding, it draws up its pointed end; and thus, creeping like a worm, will travel many feet from the parent stem. That very ingenious Mechanic Philosopher, Mr. Edgeworth, once made on this principle a wooden automaton; its back consisted of soft Fir-wood, about an inch square, and four feet long, made of pieces cut the cross-way in respect to the fibres of the wood, and glued together: it had two feet before, and two behind, which supported the back horizontally; but were placed with their extremities, which were armed with sharp points of iron, bending backwards. Hence, in moist weather, the back lengthened, and the two foremost feet were pushed forwards; in dry weather the hinder feet were drawn after, as the obliquity of the points of the feet prevented it from receding. And thus, in a month or two, it walked across the room which it inhabited. Might not this machine be applied as an Hygrometer to some meteorological purpose?]

With rage and hate the astonish'd groves alarms,
And hurls her infants from her frantic arms.
135 —So when MEDÆA left her native soil
Unaw'd by danger, unsubdued by toil;
Her weeping sire and beckoning friends withstood,
And launch'd enamour'd on the boiling flood;
One ruddy boy her gentle lips caress'd,
140 And one fair girl was pillow'd on her breast;

While high in air the golden treasure burns,
And Love and Glory guide the prow by turns.
But, when Thessalia's inauspicious plain
Received the matron-heroine from the main;
145 While horns of triumph sound, and altars burn,
And shouting nations hail their Chief's return:
Aghast, She saw new-deck'd the nuptial bed,
And proud CREUSA to the temple led;
Saw her in JASON'S mercenary arms
150 Deride her virtues, and insult her charms;
Saw her dear babes from fame and empire torn,
In foreign realms deserted and forlorn;
Her love rejected, and her vengeance braved,
By Him her beauties won, her virtues saved.—
155 With stern regard she eyed the traitor-king,
And felt, Ingratitude! thy keenest sting;
"Nor Heaven," She cried, "nor Earth, nor Hell can hold
"A Heart abandon'd to the thirst of Gold!"
Stamp'd with wild foot, and shook her horrent brow,
160 And call'd the furies from their dens below.
 —Slow out of earth, before the festive crowds,
On wheels of fire, amid a night of clouds,
Drawn by fierce fiends arose a magic car,
Received the Queen, and hovering flamed in air.—
165 As with raised hands the suppliant traitors kneel
And fear the vengeance they deserve to feel,
Thrice with parch'd lips her guiltless babes she press'd,
And thrice she clasp'd them to her tortur'd breast;
Awhile with white uplifted eyes she stood,
170 Then plung'd her trembling poniards in their blood.
"Go, kiss your sire! go, share the bridal mirth!"
She cry'd, and hurl'd their quivering limbs on earth.
Rebellowing thunders rock the marble towers,

And red-tongued lightnings shoot their arrowy showers;
175 Earth yawns!—the crashing ruin sinks!—o'er all
Death with black hands extends his mighty Pall;
Their mingling gore the Fiends of Vengeance quaff,
And Hell receives them with convulsive laugh.

Round the vex'd isles where fierce tornados roar,
180 Or tropic breezes sooth the sultry shore;
What time the eve her gauze pellucid spreads
O'er the dim flowers, and veils the misty meads;
Slow, o'er the twilight sands or leafy walks,
With gloomy dignity DICTAMNA stalks;

Spontaneous & combustion essential oils

[*Dictamnus*. l. 184. Fraxinella. In the still evenings of dry seasons this plant emits an inflammable air or gas, and flashes on the approach of a candle. There are instances of human creatures who have taken fire spontaneously, and been totally consumed. Phil. Trans.

The odours of many flowers, so delightful to our sense of smell, as well as the disgreeable scents of others, are owing to the exhalation of their essential oils. These essential oils have greater or less volatility, and are all inflammable; many of them are poisons to us, as these of Laurel and Tobacco; others possess a narcotic quality, as is evinced by the oil of cloves instantly relieving slight tooth-achs; from oil of cinnamon relieving the hiccup; and balsam of peru relieving the pain of some ulcers. They are all deleterious to certain insects, and hence their use in the vegetable economy being produced in flowers or leaves to protect them from the depredations of their voracious enemies. One of the essential oils, that of turpentine, is recommended, by M. de Thosse, for the purpose of destroying insects which infect both vegetables and animals. Having observed that the trees were attacked by multitudes of small insects of different colours (pucins ou pucerons), which injured their young branches, he destroyed them all intirely in the following manner: he put into a bowl a few handfuls of earth, on which he poured a small quantity of oil of turpentine; he then beat the whole together with a spatula, pouring on it water till it became of the consistence of soup; with this mixture he moistened the ends of the branches, and both the insects and their eggs were destroyed, and other insects kept aloof by the scent of the turpentine. He adds, that he destroyed the fleas of his puppies by once bathing them in warm water impregnated with oil of turpentine. Mem. d'Agriculture, An. 1787, Trimest. Printemp. p. 109. I sprinkled some oil of turpentine, by means of a brush, on some branches of a nectarine-tree, which was covered with the aphis; but it killed both the insect and the branches: a solution of arsenic much diluted did the same. The shops of medicine are supplied with resins, balsams, and essential oils; and the tar and pitch, for mechanical purposes, arc produced from these vegetable secretions.]

185 In sulphurous eddies round the weird dame

Plays the light gas, or kindles into flame.
If rests the traveller his weary head,
Grim MANCINELLA haunts the mossy bed,
Brews her black hebenon, and, stealing near,
190 Pours the curst venom in his tortured ear.—
Wide o'er the mad'ning throng URTICA flings
Her barbed shafts, and darts her poison'd stings.

[*Mancinella*, I. 188. Hyppomane. With the milky juice of this tree the Indians poison their arrows; the dew-drops, which fall from it, are so caustic as to blister the skin, and produce dangerous ulcers; whence many have found their death by sleeping under its shade. Variety of noxious plants abound in all countries; in our own the deadly nightshade, henbane, hounds-tongue, and many others, are seen in almost every high road untouched by animals. Some have asked, what is the use of such abundance of poisons? The nauseous or pungent juices of some vegetables, like the thorns of others, are given them for their defence from the depredations of animals; hence the thorny plants are in general wholesome and agreeable food to graminivorous animals. See note on Ilex. The flowers or petals of plants are perhaps in general more acrid than their leaves; hence they are much seldomer eaten by insects. This seems to have been the use of the essential oil in the vegetable economy, as observed above in the notes on Dictamnus and on Ilex. The fragrance of plants is thus a part of their defence. These pungent or nauseous juices of vegetables have supplied the science of medicine with its principal materials, such as purge, vomit, intoxicate, &c.]

[*Urtica*. I. 191. Nettle. The sting has a bag at its base, and a perforation near its point, exactly like the stings of wasps and the teeth of adders; Hook, Microgr. p. 142. Is the fluid contained in this bag, and pressed through the perforation into the wound, made by the point, a caustic essential oil, or a concentrated vegetable acid? The vegetable poisons, like the animal ones, produce more sudden and dangerous effects, when instilled into a wound, than when taken into the stomach; whence the families of Marfi and Psilli, in antient Rome, sucked the poison without injury out of wounds made by vipers, and were supposed to be indued with supernatural powers for this purpose. By the experiments related by Beccaria, it appears that four or five times the quantity, taken by the mouth, had about equal effects with that infused into a wound. The male flowers of the nettle are separate from the female, and the anthers are seen in fair weather to burst with force, and to discharge a dust, which hovers about the plant like a cloud.]

And fell LOBELIA'S suffocating breath
Loads the dank pinion of the gale with death.—
195 With fear and hate they blast the affrighted groves,
Yet own with tender care their *kindred Loves!*—
So, where PALMIRA 'mid her wasted plains,
Her shatter'd aqueducts, and prostrate fanes,

[*Lobelia. I.* 193. Longiflora. Grows in the West Indies, and spreads such deleterious exhalations around it, that an oppression of the breast is felt on approaching it at many feet distance when placed in the corner of a room or hot-house. Ingenhouz, Exper. on Air, p. 14.6. Jacquini hort. botanic. Vindeb. The exhalations from ripe fruit, or withering leaves, are proved much to injure the air in which they are confined; and, it is probable, all those vegetables which emit a strong scent may do this in a greater or less degree, from the Rose to the Lobelia; whence the unwholesomeness in living perpetually in such an atmosphere of perfume as some people wear about their hair, or carry in their handkerchiefs. Either Boerhaave or Dr. Mead have affirmed they were acquainted with a poisonous fluid whose vapour would presently destroy the person who sat near it. And it is well known, that the gas from fermenting liquors, or obtained from lime-stone, will destroy animals immersed in it, as well as the vapour of the Grotto del Cani near Naples.]

[*So, where Palmira. I.* 197. Among the ruins of Palmira, which are dispersed not only over the plains but even in the deserts, there is one single colonade above 2600 yards long, the bases of the Corinthian columns of which exceed the height of a man: and yet this row is only a small part of the remains of that one edifice! Volney's Travels.]

(As the bright orb of breezy midnight pours
200 Long threads of silver through her gaping towers,
     O'er mouldering tombs, and tottering columns gleams,
     And frosts her deserts with diffusive beams),
     Sad o'er the mighty wreck in silence bends,
     Lifts her wet eyes, her tremulous hands extends.—
205 If from lone cliffs a bursting rill expands
     Its transient course, and sinks into the sands;
     O'er the moist rock the fell Hyæna prowls,
     The Leopard hisses, and the Panther growls;
     On quivering wing the famish'd Vulture screams,
210 Dips his dry beak, and sweeps the gushing streams;
     With foamy jaws, beneath, and sanguine tongue,
     Laps the lean Wolf, and pants, and runs along;
     Stern stalks the Lion, on the rustling brinks
     Hears the dread Snake, and trembles as he drinks;
215 Quick darts the scaly Monster o'er the plain,
     Fold after fold, his undulating train;
     And, bending o'er the lake his crested brow,
     Starts at the Crocodile, that gapes below.

     Where seas of glass with gay reflections smile
220 Round the green coasts of Java's palmy isle;
     A spacious plain extends its upland scene,

Rocks rise on rocks, and fountains gush between;
Soft zephyrs blow, eternal summers reign,
And showers prolific bless the soil,—in vain!
225   —No spicy nutmeg scents the vernal gales,
Nor towering plaintain shades the mid-day vales;
No grassy mantle hides the sable hills,
No flowery chaplet crowns the trickling rills;
Nor tufted moss, nor leathery lichen creeps
230   In russet tapestry o'er the crumbling steeps.
  —No step retreating, on the sand impress'd,
Invites the visit of a second guest;
No refluent fin the unpeopled stream divides,
No revolant pinion cleaves the airy tides;

235   Nor handed moles, nor beaked worms return,
That mining pass the irremeable bourn.—
Fierce in dread silence on the blasted heath
Fell UPAS sits, the HYDRA-TREE of death.
Lo! from one root, the envenom'd soil below,
240   A thousand vegetative serpents grow;
In shining rays the scaly monster spreads
O'er ten square leagues his far-diverging heads;
Or in one trunk entwists his tangled form,
Looks o'er the clouds, and hisses in the storm.

[*Upas*. l. 238. There is a poison-tree in the island of Java, which is said by its effluvia to have depopulated the country for 12 or 14 miles round the place of its growth. It is called, in the Malayan language, Bohon-Upas; with the juice of it the most poisonous arrows are prepared; and, to gain this, the condemned criminals are sent to the tree with proper direction both to get the juice and to secure themselves from the malignant exhalations of the tree; and are pardoned if they bring back a certain quantity of the poison. But by the registers there kept, not one in four are said to return. Not only animals of all kinds, both quadrupeds, fish, and birds, but all kinds of vegetables also are destroyed by the effluvia of the noxious tree; so that, in a district of 12 or 14 miles round it, the face of the earth is quite barren and rocky, intermixed only with the skeletons of men and animals; affording a scene of melancholy beyond what poets have described or painters delineated. Two younger trees of its own species are said to grow near it. See London Magazine for 1784, or 1783. Translated from a description of the poison-tree of the island of Java, written in Dutch by N.P. Foereh. For a further account of it, see a note at the end of the work.]

245   Steep'd in fell poison, as his sharp teeth part,
A thousand tongues in quick vibration dart;
Snatch the proud Eagle towering o'er the heath,

Or pounce the Lion, as he stalks beneath;
Or strew, as marshall'd hosts contend in vain,
250　With human skeletons the whiten'd plain.
　　—Chain'd at his root two scion-demons dwell,
　　Breathe the faint hiss, or try the shriller yell;
　　Rise, fluttering in the air on callow wings,
　　And aim at insect-prey their little stings.
255　So Time's strong arms with sweeping scythe erase
　　Art's cumberous works, and empires, from their base;
　　While each young Hour its sickle fine employs,
　　And crops the sweet buds of domestic joys!

　　With blushes bright as morn fair ORCHIS charms,
260　And lulls her infant in her fondling arms;

[*Orchis.* l. 259. The Orchis morio in the circumstance of the parent-root shrivelling up and dying, as the young one increases, is not only analogous to other tuberous or knobby roots, but also to some bulbous roots, as the tulip. The manner of the production of herbaceous plants from their various perennial roots, seems to want further investigation, as their analogy is not yet clearly established. The caudex, or true root, in the orchis lies above the knob; and from this part the fibrous roots and the new knob are produced. In the tulip the caudex lies below the bulb; from whence proceed the fibrous roots and the new bulbs; and I suspect the tulip-root, after it has flowered, dies like the orchis-root; for the stem of the last year's tulip lies on the outside, and not in the center of the new bulb; which I am informed does not happen in the three or four first years when raised from seed, when it only produces a stem, and slender leaves without flowering. In the tulip-root, dissected in the early spring, just before it begins to shoot, a perfect flower is seen in its center; and between the first and second coat the large next year's bulb is, I believe, produced; between the second and third coat, and between this and the fourth coat, and perhaps further, other less and less bulbs are visible, all adjoining to the caudex at the bottom of the mother-bulb; and which, I am told, require as many years before they will slower, as the number of the coats with which they are covered. This annual reproduction of the tulip-root induces some florists to believe that tulip-roots never die naturally, as they lose so few of them; whereas the hyacinth-roots, I am informed, will not last above five or seven years after they have flowered.

The hyacinth-root differs from the tulip-root, as the stem of the last year's flower is always found in the center of the root, and the new off-sets arise from the caudex below the bulb, but not beneath any of the concentric coats of the root, except the external one: hence Mr. Eaton, an ingenious florist of Derby, to whom I am indebted for most of the observations in this note, concludes, that the hyacinth-root does not perish annually after it has flowered like the tulip. Mr. Eaton gave me a tulip root which had been set too deep in the earth, and the caudex had elongated itself near an inch, and the new bulb was formed above the old one, and detached from it, instead of adhering to its side.

The caudex of the ranunculus, cultivated by the florists, lies above the claw-like root; in this the old root or claws die annually, like the tulip and orchis, and the new claws, which are seen above the old ones, draw down the caudex lower into the earth. The same is said to happen to Scabiosa, or Devil's bit, and some other plants, as valerian and greater plantain; the new fibrous roots rising round the caudex above the old ones, the inferior end of the root becomes stumped, as if cut off, after the old fibres are decayed, and the caudex is drawn down into the earth by these new roots. See Arum and Tulipa.]

Soft play *Affection* round her bosom's throne,
And guards his life, forgetful of her own.
So wings the wounded Deer her headlong flight,
Pierced by some ambush'd archer of the night,
265 Shoots to the woodlands with her bounding fawn,
And drops of blood bedew the conscious lawn;
There hid in shades she shuns the cheerful day,
Hangs o'er her young, and weeps her life away.

So stood Eliza on the wood-crown'd height,
270 O'er Minden's plain, spectatress of the sight,
Sought with bold eye amid the bloody strife
Her dearer self, the partner of her life;
From hill to hill the rushing host pursued,
And view'd his banner, or believed she view'd.
275 Pleased with the distant roar, with quicker tread
Fast by his hand one lisping boy she led;
And one fair girl amid the loud alarm
Slept on her kerchief, cradled by her arm;
While round her brows bright beams of Honour dart,
280 And Love's warm eddies circle round her heart

—Near and more near the intrepid Beauty press'd,
Saw through the driving smoke his dancing crest,
Saw on his helm, her virgin-hands inwove,
Bright stars of gold, and mystic-knots of love;
285 Heard the exulting shout, "they run! they run!"
"Great GOD!" she cried, "He's safe! the battle's won!"
—A ball now hisses through the airy tides,
(Some Fury wing'd it, and some Demon guides!)
Parts the fine locks, her graceful head that deck,
290 Wounds her fair ear, and sinks into her neck;
The red stream, issuing from her azure veins,
Dyes her white veil, her ivory bosom stains.—

     —"Ah me!" she cried, and, sinking on the ground,
     Kiss'd her dear babes, regardless of the wound;
295   "Oh, cease not yet to beat, thou Vital Urn!
     "Wait, gushing Life, oh, wait my Love's return!—
     "Hoarse barks the wolf, the vulture screams from far!
     "The angel, Pity, shuns the walks of war!——
     "Oh, spare ye War-hounds, spare their tender age!—
300   "On me, on me," she cried, "exhaust your rage!"—
     Then with weak arms her weeping babes caress'd,
  And sighing hid them in her blood-stain'd vest.
     From tent to tent the impatient warrior flies,
     Fear in his heart, and frenzy in his eyes;
305   Eliza's name along the camp he calls,
     Eliza echoes through the canvas walls;
  Quick through the murmuring gloom his footsteps tread,
     O'er groaning heaps, the dying and the dead,
     Vault o'er the plain, and in the tangled wood,
310   Lo! dead Eliza weltering in her blood!—
     —Soon hears his listening son the welcome sounds,
  With open arms and sparkling eyes he bounds:—
     "Speak low," he cries, and gives his little hand,
     "Eliza sleeps upon the dew-cold sand;
315   "Poor weeping Babe with bloody fingers press'd,
     "And tried with pouting lips her milkless breast;
  "Alas! we both with cold and hunger quake—
     "Why do you weep?—Mama will soon awake."
     —"She'll wake no more!" the hopeless mourner cried
320   Upturn'd his eyes, and clasp'd his hands, and sigh'd;
     Stretch'd on the ground awhile entranc'd he lay,
  And press'd warm kisses on the lifeless clay;
     And then upsprung with wild convulsive start,
     And all the Father kindled in his heart;
325   "Oh, Heavens!" he cried, "my first rash vow forgive!
     "These bind to earth, for these I pray to live!"—
  Round his chill babes he wrapp'd his crimson vest,
     And clasp'd them sobbing to his aching breast.

     Two Harlot-Nymphs, the fair CUSCUTAS please,
330   With labour'd negligence, and studied ease;

[*Cuscuta.* l. 327. Dodder. Four males, two females. This parasite plant (the seed splitting without cotyledons), protrudes a spiral body, and not endeavouring to root itself in the earth ascends the vegetables in its vicinity, spirally W.S.E. or contrary to the movement of the sun; and absorbs its nourishment by vessels apparently inserted into its supporters. It bears no leaves, except here and there a scale, very small, membranous, and close under the branch. Lin. Spec. Plant. edit. a Reichard. Vol. I. p. 352. The Rev. T. Martyn, in his elegant letters on botany, adds, that, not content with support, where it lays hold, there it draws its nourishment; and at length, in gratitude for all this, strangles its entertainer. Let. xv. A contest for air and light obtains throughout the whole vegetable world; shrubs rise above herbs; and, by precluding the air and light from them, injure or destroy them; trees suffocate or incommode shrubs; the parasite climbing plants, as Ivy, Clematis, incommode the taller trees; and other parasites, which exist without having roots on the ground, as Misletoe, Tillandsia, Epidendrum, and the mosses and funguses, incommode them all.

Some of the plants with voluble stems ascend other plants spirally east-south-west, as Humulus, Hop, Lonicera, Honey-suckle, Tamus, black Bryony, Helxine. Others turn their spiral stems west-south-east, as Convolvulus, Corn-bind, Phaseolus, Kidney-bean, Basella, Cynanche, Euphorbia, Eupatorium. The proximate or final causes of this difference have not been investigated. Other plants are furnished with tendrils for the purpose of climbing: if the tendril meets with nothing to lay hold of in its first revolution, it makes another revolution; and so on till it wraps itself quite up like a cork-screw; hence, to a careless observer, it appears to move gradually backwards and forwards, being seen sometimes pointing eastward and sometimes westward. One of the Indian grasses, Panicum arborescens, whose stem is no thicker than a goose-quill, rises as high as the tallest trees in this contest for light and air. Spec. Plant a Reichard, Vol. I. p. 161. The tops of many climbing plants are tender from their quick growth; and, when deprived of their acrimony by boiling, are an agreeable article of food. The Hop-tops are in common use. I have eaten the tops of white Bryony, Bryonia alba, and found them nearly as grateful as Asparagus, and think this plant might be profitably cultivated as an early garden-vegetable. The Tamus (called black Bryony), was less agreeable to the taste when boiled. See Galanthus.]

> In the meek garb of modest worth disguised,
> The eye averted, and the smile chastised,
>   With sly approach they spread their dangerous charms,
>   And round their victim wind their wiry arms.
> 335 So by Scamander when LAOCOON stood,
>   Where Troy's proud turrets glitter'd in the flood,
> Raised high his arm, and with prophetic call
>   To shrinking realms announced her fatal fall;
>   Whirl'd his fierce spear with more than mortal force,
> 340 And pierced the thick ribs of the echoing horse;
>
>   Two Serpent-forms incumbent on the main,
> Lashing the white waves with redundant train,
>   Arch'd their blue necks, and (hook their towering crests,
>   And plough'd their foamy way with speckled breasts;

345   Then darting fierce amid the affrighted throngs,
      Roll'd their red eyes, and shot their forked tongues,—
    —Two daring Youths to guard the hoary sire
    Thwart their dread progress, and provoke their ire.
    Round sire and sons the scaly monsters roll'd,
350   Ring above ring, in many a tangled fold,
    Close and more close their writhing limbs surround,
    And fix with foamy teeth the envenom'd wound.
    —With brow upturn'd to heaven the holy Sage
    In silent agony sustains their rage;
355   While each fond Youth, in vain, with piercing cries
    Bends on the tortured Sire his dying eyes.
    "Drink deep, sweet youths" seductive VITIS cries,
    The maudlin tear-drop glittering in her eyes;
    Green leaves and purple clusters crown her head,
360   And the tall Thyrsus stays her tottering tread.
    —*Five* hapless swains with soft assuasive smiles
    The harlot meshes in her deathful toils;
    "Drink deep," she carols, as she waves in air
    The mantling goblet, "and forget your care."—
365   O'er the dread feast malignant Chemia scowls,
    And mingles poison in the nectar'd bowls;
    Fell Gout peeps grinning through the flimsy scene,
    And bloated Dropsy pants behind unseen;
    Wrapp'd in his robe white Lepra hides his stains,
370   And silent Frenzy writhing bites his chains.

[*Vitis*. 1. 355. Vine. Five males, one female. The juice of the ripe grape is a nutritive and agreeable food, consisting chiefly of sugar and mucilage. The chemical process of fermentation converts this sugar into spirit, converts food into poison! And it has thus become the curse of the Christian world, producing more than half of our chronical diseases; which Mahomet observed, and forbade the use of it to his disciples. The Arabians invented distillation; and thus, by obtaining the spirit of fermented liquors in a less diluted slate, added to its destructive quality. A Theory of the Diabætes and Dropsy, produced by drinking fermented or spirituous liquors, is explained in a Treatise on the inverted motions of the lymphatic system, published by Dr. Darwin. Cadell.]

    So when PROMETHEUS braved the Thunderer's ire,
    Stole from his blazing throne etherial fire,
      And, lantern'd in his breast, from realms of day
      Bore the bright treasure to his Man of clay;—
375   High on cold Caucasus by VULCAN bound,
    The lean impatient Vulture fluttering round,
    His writhing limbs in vain he twists and strains

To break or loose the adamantine chains.
The gluttonous bird, exulting in his pangs,
380   Tears his swoln liver with remorseless fangs.

[*Prometheus*, l. 369. The antient story of Prometheus, who concealed in his bosom the fire he had stolen, and afterwards had a vulture perpetually gnawing his liver, affords so apt an allegory for the effects of drinking spirituous liquors, that one should be induced to think the art of distillation, as well as some other chemical processes (such as calcining gold), had been known in times of great antiquity, and lost again. The swallowing drams cannot be better represented in hieroglyphic language than by taking fire into one's bosom; and certain it is, that the general effect of drinking fermented or spirituous liquors is an inflamed, schirrous, or paralytic liver, with its various critical or consequential diseases, as leprous eruptions on the face, gout, dropsy, epilepsy, insanity. It is remarkable, that all the diseases from drinking spirituous or fermented liquors are liable to become hereditary, even to the third generation; gradually increasing, if the cause be continued, till the family becomes extinct.]

The gentle CYCLAMEN with dewy eye
Breathes o'er her lifeless babe the parting sigh;
And, bending low to earth, with pious hands
Inhumes her dear Departed in the sands.
385   "Sweet Nursling! withering in thy tender hour,
"Oh, sleep," She cries, "and rise a fairer flower!"
—So when the Plague o'er London's gasping crowds
Shook her dank wing, and steer'd her murky clouds;
When o'er the friendless bier no rites were read,
390   No dirge slow-chanted, and no pall out-spread;
While Death and Night piled up the naked throng,
And Silence drove their ebon cars along;
Six lovely daughters, and their father, swept
To the throng'd grave CLEONE saw, and wept;

[*Cyclamen*. l. 379. Shew-bread, or Sow-bread. When the seeds are ripe, the stalk of the flower gradually twists itself spirally downwards, till it touches the ground, and forcibly penetrating the earth lodges its seeds; which are thought to receive nourishment from the parent root, as they are said not to be made to grow in any other situation.

The Trifolium subterraneum, subterraneous trefoil, is another plant, which buries its seed, the globular head of the seed penetrating the earth; which, however, in this plant may be only an attempt to conceal its seeds from the ravages of birds; for there is another trefoil, the trifolium globosum, or globular woolly-headed trefoil, which has a curious manner of concealing its seeds; the lower florets only have corols and are fertile; the upper ones wither into a kind

of wool, and, forming a bead, completely conceal the fe.
Plant, a Reichard.]

395   Her tender mind, with meek Religion fraught,
       Drank all-resigned Affliction's bitter draught;
       Alive and listening to the whisper'd groan
       Of others' woes, unconscious of her own!—
       One smiling boy, her last sweet hope, she warms
400   Hushed on her bosom, circled in her arms,—
       Daughter of woe! ere morn, in vain caress'd,
       Clung the cold Babe upon thy milkless breast,
       With feeble cries thy last sad aid required,
       Stretch'd its stiff limbs, and on thy lap expired!—
405   —Long with wide eye-lids on her Child she gazed,
       And long to heaven their tearless orbs she raised;
       Then with quick foot and throbbing heart she found
       Where Chartreuse open'd deep his holy ground;

[*Where Chartreuse.* l. 406. During the plague in London, 1665, one pit to
receive the dead was dug in the Charter-house, 40 feet long, 16 feet wide, and
about 20 feet deep; and in two weeks received 1114 bodies. During this dreadful
calamity there were instances of mothers carrying their own children to those
public graves, and of people delirious, or in despair from the loss of their
friends, who threw themselves alive into these pits. Journal of the Plague-year in
1665, printed for E. Nutt, Royal-Exchange.]

       Bore her last treasure through the midnight gloom,
410   And kneeling dropp'd it in the mighty tomb;
       "I follow next!" the frantic mourner said,
       And living plunged amid the festering dead.

       Where vast Ontario rolls his brineless tides,
       And feeds the trackless forests on his sides,
415   Fair CASSIA trembling hears the howling woods,
       And trusts her tawny children to the floods.—

[*Rolls his brineless tide.* l. 411. Some philosophers have believed that the
continent of America was not raised out of the great ocean at so early a period
of time as the other continents. One reason for this opinion was, because the
great lakes, perhaps nearly as large as the Mediterranean Sea, consist of fresh
water. And as the sea-salt seems to have its origin from the destruction of
vegetable and animal bodies, washed down by rains, and carried by rivers into
lakes or seas; it would seem that this source of sea-salt had not so long existed in
that country. There is, however, a more satisfactory way of explaining this
circumstance; which is, that the American lakes lie above the level of the ocean,

e perpetually desalited by the rivers which run through them; which
case with the Mediterranean, into which a current from the main
rpetually passes.]

ffia. l. 413. Ten males, one female. The seeds are black, the stamens gold-
ur. This is one of the American fruits, which are annually thrown on the
sts of Norway; and are frequently in so recent a state as to vegetate, when
roperly taken care of, the fruit of the anacardium, cashew-nut; of cucurbita
lagenaria, bottlegourd; of the mimosa scandens, cocoons; of the piscidia
erythrina, logwood-tree; and cocoa-nuts are enumerated by Dr. Tonning.
(Amæn. Acad. 149.) amongst these emigrant seeds. The fact is truly wonderful,
and cannot be accounted for but by the existence of under currents in the
depths of the ocean; or from vortexes of water passing from one country to
another through caverns of the earth.

Sir Hans Sloane has given an account of four kinds of seeds, which are
frequently thrown by the sea upon the coasts of the islands of the northern parts
of Scotland. Phil. Trans. abridged, Vol. III. p. 540. which seeds are natives of the
West Indies, and seem to be brought thither by the gulf-stream described below.
One of these is called, by Sir H. Sloane, Phaseolus maximus perennis, which is
often also thrown on the coast of Kerry in Ireland; another is called, in Jamaica,
Horse-eye-bean; and a third is called Niker in Jamaica. He adds, that the
Lenticula marina, or Sargosso, grows on the rocks about Jamaica, is carried by
the winds and current towards the coast of Florida, and thence into the North-
American ocean, where it lies very thick on the surface of the sea.

Thus a rapid current passes from the gulf of Florida to the N.E. along the
coast of North-America, known to seamen by the name of the GULF-
STREAM. A chart of this was published by Dr. Francklin in 1768, from the
information principally of Capt. Folger. This was confirmed by the ingenious
experiments of Dr. Blagden, published in 1781, who found that the water of the
Gulf-stream was from six to eleven degrees warmer than the water of the sea
through which it ran; which must have been occasioned by its being brought
from a hotter climate. He ascribes the origin of this current to the power of the
trade-winds, which, blowing always in the same direction, carry the waters of the
Atlantic ocean to the westward, till they are stopped by the opposing continent
on the west of the Gulf of Mexico, and are thus accumulated there, and run
down the Gulf of Florida. Philos. Trans. V. 71, p. 335. Governor Pownal has
given an elegant map of this Gulf-stream, tracing it from the Gulf of Florida
northward as far as Cape Sable in Nova Scotia, and then across the Atlantic
ocean to the coast of Africa between the Canary-islands and Senegal, increasing
in breadth, as it runs, till it occupies five or six degrees of latitude. The Governor
likewise ascribes this current to the force of the trade-winds *protruding* the waters
westward, till they are opposed by the continent, and accumulated in the Gulf of
Mexico. He very ingeniously observes, that a great eddy must be produced in the
Atlantic ocean between this Gulf-stream and the westerly current protruded by
the tropical winds, and in this eddy are found the immense fields of floating
vegetables, called Saragosa weeds, and Gulf-weeds, and some light woods, which

circulate in these vast eddies, or are occasionally dri
winds. Hydraulic and Nautical Observations by Gov
currents are mentioned by the Governor in this in?
Indian Sea, northward of the line, which are asc
Monsoons. It is probable, that in process of time
west of the Gulf of Mexico may be worn away by this
against it, by which this immense current would cease to c.
change take place in the Gulf of Mexico and West Indian
subsiding of the sea, which might probably lay all those islands int o.
them to the continent.]

      Cinctured with gold while *ten* fond brothers stand,
        And guard the beauty on her native land,

        Soft breathes the gale, the current gently moves,
420   And bears to Norway's coasts her infant-loves.
        —So the sad mother at the noon of night
     From bloody Memphis stole her silent flight;
        Wrapp'd her dear babe beneath her folded vest,
        And clasp'd the treasure to her throbbing breast,
425   With soothing whispers hushed its feeble cry,
        Pressed the soft kiss, and breathed the secret sigh.—
        —With dauntless step she seeks the winding shore,
        Hears unappall'd the glimmering torrents roar;
        With Paper-flags a floating cradle weaves,
430   And hides the smiling boy in Lotus-leaves;
        Gives her white bosom to his eager lips,
     The salt tears mingling with the milk he sips;
        Waits on the reed-crown'd brink with pious guile,
        And trusts the scaly monsters of the Nile.—

435   —Erewhile majestic from his lone abode,
        Ambassador of Heaven, the Prophet trod;
     Wrench'd the red Scourge from proud Oppression's hands,
        And broke, curst Slavery! thy iron bands.

        Hark! heard ye not that piercing cry,
440   Which shook the waves and rent the sky!—
        E'en now, e'en now, on yonder Western shores
     Weeps pale Despair, and writhing Anguish roars:
        E'en now in Afric's groves with hideous yell
        Fierce SLAVERY stalks, and slips the dogs of hell;
445   From vale to vale the gathering cries rebound,
        And sable nations tremble at the sound!—

—YE BANDS OF SENATORS! whose suffrage sways
    Britannia's realms, whom either Ind obeys;
    Who right the injured, and reward the brave,
450   Stretch your strong arm, for ye have power to save!
    Throned in the vaulted heart, his dread resort,
Inexorable CONSCIENCE holds his court;
    With still small voice the plots of Guilt alarms,
    Bares his mask'd brow, his lifted hand disarms;
455   But, wrapp'd in night with terrors all his own,
    He speaks in thunder, when the deed is done.
Hear him ye Senates! hear this truth sublime,
    "HE, WHO ALLOWS OPPRESSION, SHARES THE
        CRIME."

    No radiant pearl, which crested Fortune wears,
460   No gem, that twinkling hangs from Beauty's ears,
    Not the bright stars, which Night's blue arch adorn,
    Nor rising suns that gild the vernal morn,
    Shine with such lustre as the tear, that breaks
    For other's woe down Virtue's manly cheeks."

465   Here ceased the MUSE, and dropp'd her tuneful shell,
    Tumultuous woes her panting bosom swell,
O'er her flush'd cheek her gauzy veil she throws,
    Folds her white arms, and bends her laurel'd brows;
    For human guilt awhile the Goddess sighs,
470   And human sorrows dim celestial eyes.

INTERLUDE III.

Bookseller. Poetry has been called a sister-art both to Painting and to Music; I wish to know, what are the particulars of their relationship?

Poet. It has been already observed, that the principal part of the language of poetry consists of those words, which are expressive of the ideas, which we originally receive by the organ of sight; and in this it nearly indeed resembles painting; which can express itself in no other way, but by exciting the ideas or sensations belonging to the sense of vision. But besides this essential similitude in the language of the poetic pen and pencil, these two sisters resemble each other, if I may so say, in many of their habits and manners. The painter, to produce a strong effect, makes a few parts of his picture large, distinct, and luminous, and keeps the remainder in shadow, or even beneath its natural size and colour, to give eminence to the principal figure. This is similar to the common manner of poetic composition, where the subordinate characters are kept down, to elevate and give consequence to the hero or heroine of the piece.

In the south aile of the cathedral church at Lichfield, there is an antient monument of a recumbent figure; the head and neck of which lie on a roll of matting in a kind of niche or cavern in the wall; and about five feet distant horizontally in another opening or cavern in the wall are seen the feet and ankles, with some folds of garment, lying also on a matt; and though the intermediate space is a solid stone-wall, yet the imagination supplies the deficiency, and the whole figure seems to exist before our eyes. Does not this resemble one of the arts both of the painter and the poet? The former often shows a muscular arm amidst a group of figures, or an impassioned face; and, hiding the remainder of the body behind other objects, leaves the imagination to compleat it. The latter, describing a single feature or attitude in picturesque words, produces before the mind an image of the whole.

I remember seeing a print, in which was represented a shrivelled hand stretched through an iron grate, in the stone floor of a prison-yard, to reach at a mess of porrage, which affected me with more horrid ideas of the distress of the prisoner in the dungeon below, than could have been perhaps produced by an exhibition of the whole person. And in the following beautiful scenery from the Midsummer-night's dream, (in which I have taken the liberty to alter the place of a comma), the description of the swimming step and prominent belly bring the whole figure before our eyes with the distinctness of reality.

> When we have laugh'd to see the sails conceive,
> And grow big-bellied with the wanton wind;
> Which she with pretty and with swimming gate,

Following her womb, (then rich with my young squire),
Would imitate, and sail upon the land.

There is a third sister-feature, which belongs both to the pictorial and poetic art; and that is the making sentiments and passions visible, as it were, to the spectator; this is done in both arts by describing or portraying the effects or changes which those sentiments or passions produce upon the body. At the end of the unaltered play of Lear, there is a beautiful example of poetic painting; the old King is introduced as dying from grief for the loss of Cordelia; at this crisis, Shakespear, conceiving the robe of the king to be held together by a clasp, represents him as only saying to an attendant courtier in a faint voice, "Pray, Sir, undo this button,—thank you, Sir," and dies. Thus by the art of the poet, the oppression at the bosom of the dying King is made visible, not described in words.

B. What are the features, in which these Sister-arts do not resemble each other?

P. The ingenious Bishop Berkeley, in his Treatise on Vision, a work of great ability, has evinced, that the colours, which we see, are only a language suggesting to our minds the ideas of solidity and extension, which we had before received by the sense of touch. Thus when we view the trunk of a tree, our eye can only acquaint us with the colours or shades; and from the previous experience of the sense of touch, these suggest to us the cylindrical form, with the prominent or depressed wrinkles on it. From hence it appears, that there is the strictest analogy between colours and sounds; as they are both but languages, which do not represent their correspondent ideas, but only suggest them to the mind from the habits or associations of previous experience. It is therefore reasonable to conclude, that the more artificial arrangements of these two languages by the poet and the painter bear a similar analogy.

But in one circumstance the Pen and the Pencil differ widely from each other, and that is the quantity of Time which they can include in their respective representations. The former can unravel a long series of events, which may constitute the history of days or years; while the latter can exhibit only the actions of a moment. The Poet is happier in describing successive scenes; the Painter in representing stationary ones: both have their advantages.

Where the passions are introduced, as the Poet, on one hand, has the power gradually to prepare the mind of his reader by previous climacteric circumstances; the Painter, on the other hand, can throw stronger illumination and distinctness on the principal moment or catastrophe of the action; besides the advantage he has in using an universal language, which can be *read* in an instant of time. Thus where a great number of figures are all seen together, supporting or contrasting each other, and contributing to explain or aggrandize the principal effect, we view a picture with agreeable surprize, and contemplate it with unceasing admiration. In the representation of the sacrifice of Jephtha's Daughter, a print done from a painting of Ant. Coypel, at one glance of the eye we read all the interesting passages of the last act of a well-written tragedy; so much poetry is there condensed into a moment of time.

B. Will you now oblige me with an account of the relationship between Poetry, and her other sister, Music? P. In the poetry of our language I don't think we are to look for any thing analogous to the notes of the gamut; for, except perhaps in a few exclamations or interrogations, we are at liberty to raise or sink our voice an octave or two at pleasure, without altering the sense of the words. Hence, if either poetry or prose be read in melodious tones of voice, as is done in recitativo, or in chaunting, it must depend on the speaker, not on the writer: for though words may be selected which are less harsh than others, that is, which have fewer sudden stops or abrupt consonants amongst the vowels, or with fewer sibilant letters, yet this does not constitute melody, which consists of agreeable successions of notes referrable to the gamut; or harmony, which consists of agreeable combinations of them. If the Chinese language has many words of similar articulation, which yet signify different ideas, when spoken in a higher or lower musical note, as some travellers affirm, it must be capable of much finer effect, in respect to the audible part of poetry, than any language we are acquainted with.

There is however another affinity, in which poetry and music more nearly resemble each other than has generally been understood, and that is in their measure or time. There are but two kinds of time acknowledged in modern music, which are called *triple time*, and *common time*. The former of these is divided by bars, each bar containing three crotchets, or a proportional number of their subdivisions into quavers and semiquavers. This kind of time is analogous to the measure of our heroic or iambic verse. Thus the two following couplets are each of them divided into five bars of *triple time*, each bar consisting of two crotchets and two quavers; nor can they be divided into bars analogous to *common time* without the bars interfering with some of the crotchets, so as to divide them.

3 Soft-warbling beaks ¦ in each bright blos ¦ som move,
4 And vo ¦ cal rosebuds thrill ¦ the enchanted grove, ¦

In these lines there is a quaver and a crochet alternately in every bar, except in the last, in which *the in* make two semiquavers; the *e* is supposed by Grammarians to be cut off, which any one's ear will readily determine not to be true.

3 Life buds or breathes ¦ from Indus to ¦ the poles,

4 And the ¦ vast surface kind ¦ les, as it rolls. ¦

In these lines there is a quaver and a crotchet alternately in the first bar; a quaver, two crotchets, and a quaver, make the second bar. In the third bar there is a quaver, a crotchet, and a rest after the crotchet, that is, after the word *poles*, and two quavers begin the next line. The fourth bar consists of quavers and crotchets alternately. In the last bar there is a quaver, and a rest after it, viz. after the word *kindles*; and then two quavers and a crotchet. You will clearly perceive the truth of this, if you prick the musical characters above mentioned under the verses.

The *common time* of musicians is divided into bars, each of which contains four crotchets, or a proportional number of their subdivision into quavers and semiquavers. This kind of musical time is analogous to the dactyle verses of our language, the most popular instances of which are in Mr. Anstie's Bath-Guide. In this kind of verse the bar does not begin till after the first or second syllable; and where the verse is quite complete, and written by a good ear, these first syllables added to the last complete the bar, exactly in this also corresponding with many pieces of music;

2 Yet ¦ if one may guess by the ¦ size of his calf, Sir,
4 He ¦ weighs about twenty-three ¦ stone and a half, Sir.

2 Master ¦ Mamozet's head was not ¦ finished so soon,
4 For it ¦ took up the barber a ¦ whole afternoon.

In these lines each bar consists of a crotchet, two quavers, another crotchet, and two more quavers: which are equal to four crotchets, and, like many bars of *common time* in music, may be subdivided into two in beating time without disturbing the measure.

The following verses from Shenftone belong likewise to common time:

2/4 A | river or a sea |
Was to him a dish | of tea,
And a king | dom bread and butter.

The first and second bars consist each of a crotchet, a quaver, a crotchet, a quaver, a crotchet. The third bar consists of a quaver, two crotchets, a quaver, a crotchet. The last bar is not complete without adding the letter A, which begins the first line, and then it consists of a quaver, a crotchet, a quaver, a crotchet, two quavers.

It must be observed, that the crotchets in triple time are in general played by musicians slower than those of common time, and hence minuets are generally pricked in triple time, and country dances generally in common time. So the verses above related, which are analogous to *triple time*, are generally read slower than those analogous to *common time*; and are thence generally used for graver compositions. I suppose all the different kinds of verses to be found in our odes, which have any measure at all, might be arranged under one or other of these two musical times; allowing a note or two sometimes to precede the commencement of the bar, and occasional rests, as in musical compositions: if this was attended to by those who set poetry to music, it is probable the sound and sense would oftener coincide. Whether these musical times can be applied to the lyric and heroic verses of the Greek and Latin poets, I do not pretend to determine; certain it is, that the dactyle verse of our language, when it is ended with a double rhime, much resembles the measure of Homer and Virgil, except in the length of the lines. B. Then there is no relationship between the other two of these sister-, Painting and Music? Poetry + music

P. There is at least a mathematical relationship, or perhaps I ought rather to have said a metaphysical relationship between them. Sir Isaac Newton has observed, that the breadths of the seven primary colours in the Sun's image refracted by a prism are proportional to the seven musical notes of the gamut, or to the intervals of the eight sounds contained in an octave, that is, proportional to the following numbers:

Sol.	La.	Fa.	Sol.	La.	Mi.	Fa.	Sol.
Red.	Orange.	Yellow.	Green.	Blue.	Indigo.	Violet,	
1	1	1	1	1	1	1	
9	16	10	9	16	16	9	

Newton's Optics, Book I. part 2. prop. 3 and 6. Dr. Smith, in his Harmonics, has an explanatory note upon this happy discovery, as he terms it, of Newton. Sect. 4. Art. 7. From this curious coincidence, it has been proposed to produce a luminous music, confiding of successions or combinations of colours, analogous to a tune in respect to the proportions above mentioned. This might be performed by a strong light, made by means of Mr. Argand's lamps, passing through coloured glasses, and falling on a defined part of a wall, with moveable blinds before them, which might communicate with the keys of a harpsichord; and thus produce at the same time visible and audible music in unison with each other. The execution of this idea is said by Mr. Guyot to have been attempted by Father Cassel without much success. If this should be again attempted, there is another curious coincidence between sounds and colours, discovered by Dr. Darwin of Shrewsbury, and explained in a paper on what he calls Ocular Spectra, in the Philosophical Transactions, Vol. LXXVI. which might much facilitate the execution of it. In this treatise the Doctor has demonstrated, that we see certain colours, not only with greater ease and distinctness, but with relief and pleasure, after having for some time contemplated other certain colours; as green after red, or red after green; orange after blue, or blue after orange; yellow after violet, or violet after yellow. This he shews arises from the *ocular spectrum* of the colour last viewed coinciding with the *irritation* of the colour now under contemplation. Now as the pleasure we receive from the sensation of melodious notes, independent of the previous associations of agreeable ideas with them, must arise from our hearing some proportions of sounds after others more easily, distinctly, or agreeably; and as there is a coincidence between the proportions of the primary colours, and the primary sounds, if they may be so called; he argues, that the same laws must govern the sensations of both. In this circumstance, therefore, consists the sisterhood of Music and Painting; and hence they claim a right to borrow metaphors from each other; musicians to speak of the brilliancy of sounds, and the light and shade of a concerto; and painters of the harmony of colours, and the tone of a picture. Thus it was not quite so absurd, as was imagined, when the blind man asked if the colour scarlet was like the sound of a trumpet. As the coincidence or opposition of these *ocular spectra*, (or colours which remain in the eye after having for some time contemplated a luminous object) are more easily and more accurately ascertained, now their laws have been investigated by Dr. Darwin, than the *relicts* of evanescent sounds upon the ear; it is to be wished that some ingenious musician would further cultivate this curious field of science: for if visible music can be agreeably produced, it would be more easy to add sentiment to it by the representations of groves and Cupids, and sleeping nymphs amid the changing colours, than is commonly done by the words of audible music.

B. You mentioned the greater length of the verses of Homer and Virgil. Had not these poets great advantage in the superiority of their languages compared to our own?

P. It is probable, that the introduction of philosophy into a country must gradually affect the language of it; as philosophy converses in more appropriated and abstracted terms; and thus by degrees eradicates the abundance of metaphor, which is used in the more early ages of society. Otherwise, though the Greek compound words have more vowels in proportion to their consonants than the English ones, yet the modes of compounding them are less general; as may be seen by variety of instances given in the preface of the Translators, prefixed to the SYSTEM OF VEGETABLES by the Lichfield Society; which happy property of our own language rendered that translation of Linneus as expressive and as concise, perhaps more so than the original.

And in one respect, I believe, the English language serves the purpose of poetry better than the antient ones, I mean in the greater ease of producing personifications; for as our nouns have in general no genders affixed to them in prose-compositions, and in the habits of conversation, they become easily personified only by the addition of a masculine or feminine pronoun, as,

> Pale Melancholy sits, and round *her* throws
> A death-like silence, and a dread repose.
> *Pope's Abelard.*

And secondly, as most of our nouns have the article *a* or *the* prefixed to them in prose-writing and in conversation, they in general become personified even by the omission of these articles; as in the bold figure of Shipwreck in Miss Seward's Elegy on Capt. Cook:

> But round the steepy rocks and dangerous strand
> Rolls the white surf, and SHIPWRECK guards the land.

Add to this, that if the verses in our heroic poetry be shorter than those of the ancients, our words likewise are shorter; and in respect to their measure or time, which has erroneously been called melody and harmony, I doubt, from what has been said above, whether we are so much inferior as is generally believed; since many passages, which have been stolen from antient poets, have been translated into our language without losing any thing of the beauty of the versification.

B. I am glad to hear you acknowledge the thefts of the modern poets from the antient ones, whose works I suppose have been reckoned lawful plunder in all ages. But have not you borrowed epithets, phrases, and even half a line occasionally from modern poems?

P. It may be difficult to mark the exact boundary of what should be termed plagiarism: where the sentiment and expression are both borrowed without due acknowledgement, there can be no doubt;—single words, on the contrary, taken from other authors, cannot convict a writer of plagiarism; they are lawful game, wild by nature, the property of all who can capture them;—and perhaps a few common flowers of speech may be gathered, as we pass over our neighbour's inclosure, without stigmatizing us with the title of thieves; but we must not therefore plunder his cultivated fruit.

The four lines at the end of the plant Upas are imitated from Dr. Young's Night Thoughts. The line in the episode adjoined to Cassia, "The salt tear mingling with the milk he sips," is from an interesting and humane passage in Langhorne's Justice of Peace. There are probably many others, which, if I could recollect them, should here be acknowledged. As it is, like exotic plants, their mixture with the natives ones, I hope, adds beauty to my Botanic Garden:—and such as it is, *Mr. Bookseller,* I now leave it to you to desire the Ladies and Gentlemen to walk in; but please to apprize them, that, like the spectators at an unskilful exhibition in some village-barn, I hope they will make Good-humour one of their party; and thus theirselves supply the defects of the representation.

THE LOVES OF THE PLANTS

CANTO IV.

Now the broad Sun his golden orb unshrouds,
Flames in the west, and paints the parted clouds;
O'er heaven's wide arch refracted lustres flow,
And bend in air the many-colour'd bow.—
5   —The tuneful Goddess on the glowing sky
Fix'd in mute extacy her glistening eye:
And then her lute to sweeter tones she strung,
And swell'd with softer chords the Paphian song.
Long ailes of Oaks return'd the silver sound,
10   And amorous Echoes talk'd along the ground;
Pleas'd Lichfield listen'd from her sacred bowers,
Bow'd her tall groves, and shook her stately towers.

"Nymph! not for thee the radiant day returns,
Nymph! not for thee the golden solstice burns,
15   Refulgent CEREA!—at the dusky hour
She seeks with pensive step the mountain-bower,

[*Pleas'd Lichfield.* l. 11. The scenery described at the beginning of the first part, or economy of vegetation, is taken from a botanic garden about a mile from Lichfield.

Cerea. l. 15. Cactus grandiflorus, or Cereus. Twenty males, one female. This flower is a native of Jamaica and Veracrux. It expands a most exquisitely beautiful corol, and emits a most fragrant odour for a few hours in the night, and then closes to open no more. The flower is nearly a foot in diameter; the inside of the calyx of a splendid yellow, and the numerous petals of a pure white: it begins to open about seven or eight o'clock in the evening, and closes before sun-rise in the morning. Martyn's Letters, p. 294. The Cistus labdiniferus, and many other flowers, lose their petals after having been a few hours expanded in the day-time; for in these plants the stigma is soon impregnated by the numerous anthers: in many flowers of the Cistus lubdiniferus I observed two or three of the stamens were perpetually bent into contact with the pistil.

The Nyctanthes, called Arabian Jasmine, is another flower, which expands a beautiful corol, and gives out a most delicate perfume during the night, and not in the day, in its native country, whence its name; botanical philosophers have not yet explained this wonderful property; perhaps the plant sleeps during the day as some animals do; and its odoriferous glands only emit their fragrance during the expansion of the petals; that is, during its waking hours: the Geranium triste has the same property of giving up its fragrance only in the night. The flowers of the Cucurbita lagenaria are said to close when the sun shines upon them. In our climate many flowers, as tragopogon, and hibiscus, close their flowers before the hottest part of the day comes on; and the flowers of some species of cucubalus, and Silene, viscous campion, are closed all day; but when the sun leaves them they expand, and emit a very agreeable scent; whence such plants are termed noctiflora.]

Bright as the blush of rising morn, and warms
The dull cold eye of Midnight with her charms.
There to the skies she lifts her pencill'd brows,
20 Opes her fair lips, and breathes her virgin vows;
Eyes the white zenyth; counts the suns, that roll
Their distant fires, and blaze around the Pole;
Or marks where Jove directs his glittering car
O'er Heaven's blue vault,—Herself a brighter star.
25 —There as soft Zephyrs sweep with pausing airs
Thy snowy neck, and part thy shadowy hairs,
Sweet Maid of Night! to Cynthia's sober beams
Glows thy warm cheek, thy polish'd bosom gleams.
In crowds around thee gaze the admiring swains,
30 And guard in silence the enchanted plains;
Drop the still tear, or breathe the impassion'd sigh,
And drink inebriate rapture from thine eye.
Thus, when old Needwood's hoary scenes the Night
Paints with blue shadow, and with milky light;
35 Where MUNDY pour'd, the listening nymphs among,
Loud to the echoing vales his parting song;
With measured step the Fairy Sovereign treads,
Shakes her high plume, and glitters o'er the meads;
Round each green holly leads her sportive train,
40 And little footsteps mark the circled plain;
Each haunted rill with silver voices rings,
And Night's sweet bird in livelier accents sings.

Ere the bright star, which leads the morning sky,
Hangs o'er the blushing east his diamond eye,
45 The chaste TROPAEO leaves her secret bed;
A saint-like glory trembles round her head;

[*Where Mundy.* l. 35. Alluding to an unpublished poem by F. N. Mundy, Esq. on his leaving Needwood-Forest.

Tropæolum. l. 45. Majus. Garden Nasturtion, or greater Indian cress. Eight males, one female. Miss E. C. Linneus first observed the Tropæolum Majus to emit sparks or flashes in the mornings before sun-rise, during the months of June or July, and also during the twilight in the evening, but not after total darkness came on; these singular scintillations were shewn to her father and other philosophers; and Mr. Wilcke, a celebrated electrician, believed them to be electric. Lin. Spec. Plantar. p. 490. Swedish Acts for the year 1762. Pulteney's View of Linneus, p. 220. Nor is this more wonderful than that the electric eel and torpedo should give voluntary shocks of electricity; and in this plant perhaps, as in those animals, it may be a mode of defence, by which it harrasses or destroys the night-flying insects which infest it; and probably it may emit the same sparks during the day, which must be then invisible. This curious subject deserves further investigation. See Dictamnus. The ceasing to shine of this plant after twilight might induce one to conceive, that it absorbed and emitted light, like the Bolognian Phosphorus, or calcined oyster-shells, so well explained by Mr. B. Wilson, and by T. B. Beccari. Exper. on Phosphori, by B. Wilson. Dodsley. The light of the evening, at the same distance from noon, is much greater, as I have repeatedly observed, than the light of the morning: this is owing, I suppose, to the phosphorescent quality of almost all bodies, in a greater or less degree, which thus absorb light during the sun-shine, and continue to emit it again for some time afterwards, though not in such quantity as to produce apparent scintillations. The nectary of this plant grows from what is supposed to be the calyx; but this supposed calyx is coloured; and perhaps, from this circumstance of its bearing the nectary, should rather be esteemed a part of the coral. See an additional note at the end of the poem.]

> *Eight* watchful swains along the lawns of night
> With amorous steps pursue the virgin light;
> O'er her fair form the electric lustre plays,
> 50 And cold she moves amid the lambent blaze.
> So shines the glow-fly, when the sun retires,
> And gems the night-air with phosphoric fires;

[*So shines the glow-fly.* l. 52. In Jamaica, in some seasons of the year, the fire-flies are seen in the evenings in great abundance. When they settle on the ground, the bull-frog greedily devours them; which seems to have given origin to a curious, though cruel, method of destroying these animals: if red-hot pieces of charcoal be thrown towards them in the dusk of the evening, they leap at them, and, hastily swallowing them, are burnt to death.]

> Thus o'er the marsh aërial lights betray,
> And charm the unwary wanderer from his way.
> 55 So when thy King, Assyria, fierce and proud,
> Three human victims to his idol vow'd;
> Rear'd a vast pyre before the golden shrine
> Of sulphurous coal, and pitch-exsuding pine;—
> —Loud roar the flames, the iron nostrils breathe,
> 60 And the huge bellows pant and heave beneath;
> Bright and more bright the blazing deluge flows,
> And white with seven-fold heat the furnace glows.
> And now the Monarch fix'd with dread surprize

Deep in the burning vault his dazzled eyes.
65   "Lo! Three unbound amid the frightful glare,
Unscorch'd their sandals, and unsing'd their hair!
And now a fourth with seraph-beauty bright
Descends, accosts them, and outshines the light!
Fierce flames innocuous, as they step, retire!
70   And slow they move amid a world of fire!"
He spoke,—to Heaven his arms repentant spread,
And kneeling bow'd his gem-incircled head.
Two Sister-Nymphs, the fair AVENAS, lead
Their fleecy squadrons on the lawns of Tweed;
75   Pass with light step his wave-worn banks along,
And wake his Echoes with their silver tongue;
Or touch the reed, as gentle Love inspires,
In notes accordant to their chaste desires.

I.

"Sweet ECHO! sleeps thy vocal shell,
"Where this high arch o'erhangs the dell;
"While Tweed with sun-reflecting streams
"Chequers thy rocks with dancing beams?—

[*Ovena.* l. 73. Oat. The numerous families of grasses have all three males, and two females, except Anthoxanthum, which gives the grateful smell to hay, and has but two males. The herbs of this order of vegetables support the countless tribes of graminivorous animals. The seeds of the smaller kinds of grasses, as of aira, poa, briza, stipa, &c. are the sustenance of many sorts of birds. The seeds of the large grasses, as of wheat, barley, rye, oats, supply food to the human species.

It seems to have required more ingenuity to think of feeding nations of mankind with so small a seed, than with the potatoe of Mexico, or the bread-fruit of the southern islands; hence Ceres in Egypt, which was the birth-place of our European arts, was deservedly celebrated amongst their divinities, as well as Osyris, who invented the Plough.

Mr. Wahlborn observes, that as wheat, rye, and many of the grasses, and plantain, lift up their anthers on long filments, and thus expose the enclosed fecundating dust to be washed away by the rains, a scarcity of corn is produced by wet summers; hence the necessity of a careful choice of seed wheat, as that, which had not received the dust of the anthers, will not grow, though it may appear well to the eye. The straw of the oat seems to have been the first musical instrument, invented during the pastoral ages of the world, before the discovery of metals. See note on Cistus.]

II.

"Here may no clamours harsh intrude,
No brawling hound or clarion rude;
85   Here no fell beast of midnight prowl,
And teach thy tortured cliffs to howl!

III.

"Be thine to pour these vales along
Some artless Shepherd's evening song;
While Night's sweet bird, from yon high spray
90   Responsive, listens to his lay.

IV.

"And if, like me, some love-lorn maid
"Should sing her sorrows to thy shade,
"Oh, sooth her breast, ye rocks around!
"With softest sympathy of sound."

95   From ozier bowers the brooding Halcyons peep,
The Swans pursuing cleave the glassy deep,
On hovering wings the wondering Reed-larks play,
And silent Bitterns listen to the lay.—
Three shepherd-swains beneath the beechen shades
100   Twine rival garlands for the tuneful maids;
On each smooth bark the mystic love-knot frame,
Or on white sands inscribe the favour'd name.

From Time's remotest dawn where China brings
In proud succession all her Patriot-Kings;
105   O'er desert-sands, deep gulfs, and hills sublime,
Extends her massy wall from clime to clime;
With bells and dragons crests her Pagod-bowers,
Her silken palaces, and porcelain towers;
With long canals a thousand nations laves;
110   Plants all her wilds, and peoples all her waves;
Slow treads fair CANNABIS the breezy strand,
The distaff streams dishevell'd in her hand;

[*Cannabis*. l. 111. Chinese Hemp. Two houses. Five males. A new species of hemp, of which an account is given by K. Fitzgerald, Esq. in a letter to Sir Joseph Banks, and which is believed to be much superior to the hemp of other countries. A few seeds of this plant were sown in England on the 4th of June, and grew to fourteen feet seven inches in height by the middle of October; they were nearly seven inches in circumference, and bore many lateral branches, and produced very white and tough fibres. At some parts of the time these plants grew nearly eleven inches in a week. Philos. Trans. Vol. LXXII. p. 46.]

> Now to the left her ivory neck inclines,
> And leads in Paphian curves its azure lines;
> 115 Dark waves the fringed lid, the warm cheek glows,
> And the fair ear the parting locks disclose;
> Now to the right with airy sweep she bends,
> Quick join the threads, the dancing spole depends.
> —*Five* Swains attracted guard the Nymph, by turns
> 120 Her grace inchants them, and her beauty burns;
> To each She bows with sweet assuasive smile,
> Hears his soft vows, and turns her spole the while.
>
> So when with light and shade, concordant strife!
> Stern CLOTHO weaves the chequer'd thread of life;
> 125 Hour after hour the growing line extends,
> The cradle and the coffin bound its ends;

[*Paphian curves.* l. 114. In his ingenious work, entitled, The Analysis of Beauty, Mr. Hogarth believes that the triangular glass, which was dedicated to Venus in her temple at Paphos, contained in it a line bending spirally round a cone with a certain degree of curviture; and that this pyramidal outline and serpentine curve constitute the principles of Grace and Beauty.]

> Soft cords of silk the whirling spoles reveal,
> If smiling Fortune turn the giddy wheel;
> But if sweet Love with baby-fingers twines,
> 130 And wets with dewy lips the lengthening lines,
> Skein after skein celestial tints unfold,
> And all the silken tissue shines with gold.
>
> Warm with sweet blushes bright GALANTHA glows,
> And prints with frolic step the melting snows;

[*Galanthus.* l. 133. Nivalis. Snowdrop. Six males, one female. The first flower that appears after the winter solstice. See Stillingfleet's Calendar of Flora.

Some snowdrop-roots taken up in winter, and boiled, had the insipid mucilaginous taste of the Orchis, and, if cured in the same manner, would probably make as good salep. The roots of the Hyacinth, I am informed, are equally insipid, and might be used as an article of food. Gmelin, in his History of Siberia, says the Martigon Lily makes a part of the food of that country, which is of the same natural order as the snowdrop. Some roots of Crocus, which I boiled, had a disagreeable flavour.

The difficulty of raising the Orchis from seed has, perhaps, been a principal reason of its not being cultivated in this country as an article of food. It is affirmed, by one of the Linnean school, in the Amoenit. Academ. that the seeds of Orchis will ripen, if you destroy the new bulb; and that Lily of the Valley, Convallaria, will produce many more seeds, and ripen them, if the roots be crowded in a garden-pot, so as to prevent them from producing many bulbs. Vol. VI. p. 120. It is probable either of these methods may succeed with these and other bulbous-rooted plants, as snowdrops, and might render their cultivation profitable in this climate. The root of the asphodelus ramosus, branchy asphodel, is used to feed swine in France; and starch is obtained from the alstromeria licta. Memoires d'Agricult.]

135 O'er silent floods, white hills, and glittering meads
      Six rival swains the playful beauty leads,
      Chides with her dulcet voice the tardy Spring,
      Bids slumbering Zephyr stretch his folded wing,
      Wakes the hoarse Cuckoo in his gloomy cave,
140 And calls the wondering Dormouse from his grave,
      Bids the mute Redbreast cheer the budding grove,
      And plaintive Ringdove tune her notes to love.

      Spring! with thy own sweet smile, and tuneful tongue,
      Delighted BELLIS calls her infant throng.
145 Each on his reed astride, the Cherub-train
      Watch her kind looks, and circle o'er the plain;
      Now with young wonder touch the sliding snail,
      Admire his eye-tipp'd horns, and painted mail;
      Chase with quick step, and eager arms outspread,
150 The pausing Butterfly from mead to mead;

[*Bellis prolifera* l. 144. Hen and chicken Daisy; in this beautiful monster not only the impletion or doubling of the petals takes place, as described in the note on Alcea; but a numerous circlet of less flowers on peduncles, or footstalks, rise from the sides of the calyx, and surround the proliferous parent. The same occurs in Calendula, marigold; in Heracium, hawk-weed; and in Scabiosa, Scabious. Phil. Botan. p. 82.]

      Or twine green oziers with the fragrant gale,
      The azure harebel, and the primrose pale,
      Join hand in hand, and in procession gay
      Adorn with votive wreaths the shrine of May.
155 —So moves the Goddess to the Idalian groves,
      And leads her gold-hair'd family of Loves.

These, from the flaming furnace, strong and bold
Pour the red steel into the sandy mould;
On tinkling anvils (with Vulcanian art),
160 Turn with hot tongs, and forge the dreadful dart;
The barbed head on whirling jaspers grind,
And dip the point in poison for the mind;
Each polish'd shaft with snow-white plumage wing,
Or strain the bow reluctant to its string.
165 Those on light pinion twine with busy hands,
Or stretch from bough to bough the flowery bands;

[*The fragrant Gale.* l. 151. The buds of the Myrica Gale possess an agreeable aromatic fragrance, and might be worth attending to as an article of the Materia Medica. Mr. Sparman suspects, that the green wax-like substance, with which at certain times of the year the berries of the Myrica cerifera, or candle-berry Myrtle, are covered, are deposited there by insects. It is used by the inhabitants for making candles, which he says burn rather better than those made of tallow. *Voyage to the Cape*, V. I. 345.]

Scare the dark beetle, as he wheels on high,
Or catch in silken nets the gilded fly;
Call the young Zephyrs to their fragrant bowers,
170 And stay with kisses sweet the Vernal Hours.
Where, as proud Masson rises rude and bleak,
And with mishapen turrets crests the Peak,
Old Matlock gapes with marble jaws, beneath,
And o'er scar'd Derwent bends his flinty teeth;
175 Deep in wide caves below the dangerous soil
Blue sulphurs flame, imprison'd waters boil.

[*Deep in wide caves.* l. 175. The arguments which tend to shew that the warm springs of this country are produced from steam raised by deep subterranean fires, and afterwards condensed between the strata of the mountains, appear to me much more conclusive, than the idea of their being warmed by chemical combinations near the surface of the earth: for, 1st, their heat has kept accurately the same perhaps for many centuries, certainly as long as we have been possessed of good thermometers; which cannot be well explained, without supposing that they are first in a boiling state. For as the heat of boiling water is 212, and that of the internal parts of the earth 48, it is easy to understand, that the steam raised from boiling water, after being condensed in some mountain, and passing from thence through a certain space of the cold earth, must be cooled always to a given degree; and it is probable the distance from the exit of the spring, to the place where the steam is condensed, might be guessed by the degree of its warmth.

2. In the dry summer of 1780, when all other springs were either dry or much diminished, those of Buxton and Matlock (as I was well informed on the spot), had suffered no diminution; which proves that the sources of these warm springs are at great depths below the surface of the earth.

3. There are numerous perpendicular fissures in the rocks of Derbyshire, in which the ores of lead and copper are found, and which pass to unknown depths; and might thence afford a passage to steam from great subterraneous fires.

4. If these waters were heated by the decomposition of pyrites, there would be some chalybeate taste or sulphureous smell in them. See note in part 1. on the existence of central fires.]

> Impetuous steams in spiral colums rise
> Through rifted rocks, impatient for the skies;
> Or o'er bright seas of bubbling lavas blow,
> 180 As heave and toss the billowy fires below;
> Condensed on high, in wandering rills they glide
> From Masson's dome, and burst his sparry side;
> Round his grey towers, and down his fringed walls,
> From cliff to cliff, the liquid treasure falls;
> 185 In beds of stalactite, bright ores among,
> O'er corals, shells, and crystals, winds along;
> Crusts the green mosses, and the tangled wood,
> And sparkling plunges to its parent flood.
> —O'er the warm wave a smiling youth presides,
> 190 Attunes its murmurs, its meanders guides,
>
> (The blooming FUCUS), in her sparry coves
> To amorous Echo sings his *secret* loves,
> Bathes his fair forehead in the misty stream,
> And with sweet breath perfumes the rising steam.
> 195 —So, erst, an Angel o'er Bethesda's springs,
> Each morn descending, shook his dewy wings;
> And as his bright translucent form He laves,
> Salubrious powers enrich the troubled waves.

[*Fucus*.l. 191. Clandestine marriage. A species of Fucus, or of Conserva, soon appears in all basons which contain water. Dr. Priestley found that great quantities of pure dephlogisticated air were given up in water at the points of this vegetable, particularly in the sunshine, and that hence it contributed to preserve the water in reservoirs from becoming putrid. The minute divisions of the leaves of subaquatic plants, as mentioned in the note on Trapa, and of the gills of fish, seem to serve another purpose besides that of increasing their surface, which has not, I believe, been attended to, and that is to facilitate the separation of the air, which is mechanically mixed or chemically dissolved in water by their points or edges; this appears on immersing a dry hairy leaf in water fresh from a pump; innumerable globules like quicksilver appear on almost every point; for the extremities of these points attract the particles of water less forcibly than those particles attract each other; hence the contained air, whose elasticity was but just balanced by the attractive power of the surrounding particles of water to each other, finds at the point of each fibre a place where the resistance to its expansion is less; and in consequence it there expands, and becomes a bubble of air. It is easy to foresee that the rays of the sunshine, by being refracted and in part relieved by the two surfaces of these minute air-bubbles, must impart to them much more heat than to the transparent water; and thus facilitate their ascent by further expanding them; that the points of vegetables attract the particles of water less than they attract each other, is seen by the spherical form of dew-drops on the points of grass. See note on Vegetable Respiration in Part I.]

> Amphibious Nymph, from Nile's prolific bed
> 200   Emerging TRAPA lifts her pearly head;
> Fair glows her virgin cheek and modest breast,
> A panoply of scales deforms the rest;

[*Trapa*, l. 200. Four males, one female. The lower leaves of this plant grow under water, and are divided into minute capillary ramifications; while the upper leaves are broad and round, and have air-bladders in their footstalks to support them above the surface of the water. As the aerial leaves of vegetables do the office of lungs, by exposing a large surface of vessels with their contained fluids to the influence of the air; so these aquatic leaves answer a similar purpose like the gills of fish; and perhaps gain from water or give to it a similar material. As the material thus necessary to life seems to abound more in air than in water, the subaquatic leaves of this plant, and of sisymbrium, coenanthe, ranunculus aquatilis, water crowfoot, and some others, are cut into fine divisions to increase the surface; whilst those above water are undivided. So the plants on high mountains have their upper leaves more divided, as pimpinella, petroselinum, and others, because here the air is thinner, and thence a larger surface of contact is required. The stream of water also passes but once along the gills of fish, as it is sooner deprived of its virtue; whereas the air is both received and ejected by the action of the lungs of land-animals. The whale seems to be an exception to the above, as he receives water and spouts it out again from an organ, which I suppose to be a respiratory one. As spring-water is nearly of the same degree of heat in all climates, the aquatic plants, which grow in rills or fountains, are found equally in the torrid, temperate, and frigid zones, as water-cress, water-parsnip, ranunculus, and many others.

In warmer climates the watery grounds are usefully cultivated, as with rice; and the roots of some aquatic plants are said to have supplied food, as the ancient Lotus in Egypt, which some have supposed to be the Nymphæa.—In Siberia the roots of the Butemus, or flowering rush, are eaten, which is well worth further enquiry, as they grow spontaneously in our ditches and rivers, which at present produce no esculent vegetables; and might thence become an article of useful cultivation. Herodotus affirms, that the Egyptian Lotus grows in the Nile, and resembles a Lily. That the natives dry it in the sun, and take the pulp out of it, which grows like the head of a poppy, and bake it for bread. Enterpe. Many grit-stones and coals, which I have seen, seem to bear an impression of the roots of the Nymphæa, which are often three or four inches thick, especially the white-flowered one.]

> Her quivering fins and panting gills she hides
> But spreads her silver arms upon the tides;
> 205 Slow as she sails, her ivory neck she laves,
> And shakes her golden tresses o'er the waves.
> Charm'd round the Nymph, in circling gambols glide
> *Four* Nereid-forms, or shoot along the tide;
> Now all as one they rise with frolic spring,
> 210 And beat the wondering air on humid wing;
> Now all descending plunge beneath the main,
> And lash the foam with undulating train;
> Above, below, they wheel, retreat, advance,
> In air and ocean weave the mazy dance;
> 215 Bow their quick heads, and point their diamond eyes,
> And twinkle to the sun with ever-changing dyes.
>
> Where Andes, crested with volcanic beams,
> Sheds a long line of light on Plata's streams;
> Opes all his springs, unlocks his golden caves,
> 220 And feeds and freights the immeasurable waves;
> Delighted OCYMA at twilight hours
> Calls her light car, and leaves the sultry bowers;—
> Love's rising ray, and Youth's seductive dye,
> Bloom'd on her cheek, and brighten'd in her eye;
> 225 Chaste, pure, and white, a zone of silver graced
> Her tender breast, as white, as pure, as chaste;—

[*Ocymum salinun*. l. 221. Saline Basil. Class Two Powers. The Abbè Molina, in his History of Chili, translated from the Italian by the Abbè Grewvel, mentions a species of Basil, which he calls Ocymum salinum: he says it resembles the common basil, except that the stalk is round and jointed; and that though it grows 60 miles from the sea, yet every morning it is covered with saline globules, which are hard and splendid, appearing at a distance like dew; and that each plant furnishes about half an ounce of fine salt every day, which the peasants collect, and use as common salt, but esteem it superior in flavour.

As an article of diet, salt seems to act simply as a stimulus, not containing any nourishment, and is the only fossil substance which the caprice of mankind has yet taken into their stomachs along with their food; and, like all other unnatural stimuli, is not necessary to people in health, and contributes to weaken our system; though it may be useful as a medicine. It seems to be the immediate cause of the sea-scurvy, as those patients quickly recover by the use of fresh provisions; and is probably a remote cause of scrophula (which consists in the want of irritability in the absorbent vessels), and is therefore serviceable to these patients; as wine is necessary to those whose stomachs have been weakened by its use. The universality of the use of salt with our food, and in our cookery, has rendered it difficult to prove the truth of these observations. I suspect that flesh-meat cut into thin slices, either raw or boiled, might be preserved in coarse sugar or treacle; and thus a very nourishing and salutary diet might be presented to our seamen. See note on Salt-rocks, in Vol. I, Canto II. If a person unaccustomed to much salt should eat a couple of red-herrings, his insensible perspiration will be so much increased by the stimulus of the salt, that he will find it necessary in about two hours to drink a quart of water: the effects of a continued use of salt in weakening the action of the lymphatic system may hence be deduced.]

By *four* fond swains in playful circles drawn,
On glowing wheels she tracks the moon-bright lawn,
Mounts the rude cliff, unveils her blushing charms,
230 And calls the panting zephyrs to her arms.
Emerged from ocean springs the vaporous air,
Bathes her light limbs, uncurls her amber hair,
Incrusts her beamy form with films saline,
And Beauty blazes through the crystal shrine.—
235 So with pellucid studs the ice-flower gems
Her rimy foliage, and her candied stems.
So from his glassy horns, and pearly eyes,
The diamond-beetle darts a thousand dyes;
Mounts with enamel'd wings the vesper gale,
240 And wheeling shines in adamantine mail.

Thus when loud thunders o'er Gomorrah burst,
And heaving earthquakes shook his realms accurst,
An Angel-guest led forth the trembling Fair
With shadowy hand, and warn'd the guiltless pair;

[*Ice-flower*. l. 235. Mesembryanthemum crystallinum.]

245 "Haste from these lands of sin, ye Righteous! fly,
Speed the quick step, nor turn the lingering eye!"—
—Such the command, as fabling Bards indite,
When Orpheus charm'd the grisly King of Night;
Sooth'd the pale phantoms with his plaintive lay,
250 And led the fair Assurgent into day.—

Wide yawn'd the earth, the fiery tempest flash'd,
And towns and towers in one vast ruin crash'd;—
Onward they move,—loud horror roars behind,
And shrieks of Anguish bellow in the wind.
255 With many a sob, amid a thousand fears,
The beauteous wanderer pours her gushing tears;
Each soft connection rends her troubled breast,
—She turns, unconscious of the stern behest!—
"I faint!—I fall!—ah, me!—sensations chill
260 Shoot through my bones, my shuddering bosom thrill!
I freeze! I freeze! just Heaven regards my fault,
Numbs my cold limbs, and hardens into salt!—
Not yet, not yet, your dying Love resign!—
This last, last kiss receive!—no longer thine!"—
265 She said, and ceased,—her stiffen'd form He press'd,
And strain'd the briny column to his breast;
Printed with quivering lips the lifeless snow,
And wept, and gazed the monument of woe.—
So when Aeneas through the flames of Troy
270 Bore his pale fire, and led his lovely boy;
With loitering step the fair Creusa stay'd,
And Death involved her in eternal shade.—
Oft the lone Pilgrim that his road forsakes,
Marks the wide ruins, and the sulphur'd lakes;
275 On mouldering piles amid asphaltic mud
Hears the hoarse bittern, where Gomorrah stood;
Recalls the unhappy Pair with lifted eye,
Leans on the crystal tomb, and breathes the silent sigh..

With net-wove sash and glittering gorget dress'd,
280 And scarlet robe lapell'd upon her breast,
Stern ARA frowns, the measured march assumes,
Trails her long lance, and nods her shadowy plumes;

[*Arum*. I. 281. Cuckow-pint, of the class Gynandria, or masculine ladies. The pistil, or female part of the flower, rises like a club, is covered above or clothed, as it were, by the anthers or males; and some of the species have a large scarlet blotch in the middle of every leaf.

The singular and wonderful structure of this flower has occasioned many disputes amongst botanists. See Tourniff. Malpig. Dillen. Rivin. &c. The receptacle is enlarged into a naked club, with the germs at its base; the stamens are affixed to the receptacle amidst the germs (a natural prodigy), and thus do not need the assistance of elevating filaments: hence the flower may be said to be inverted. *Families of Plants* translated from Linneus, p. 618.

The spadix of this plant is frequently quite white, or coloured, and the leaves liable to be streaked with white, and to have black or scarlet blotches on them. As the plant has no corol or blossom, it is probable the coloured juices in these parts of the sheath or leaves may serve the same purpose as the coloured juices in the petals of other flowers; from which I suppose the honey to be prepared. See note on Helleborus. I am informed that those tulip-roots which have a red cuticle produce red flowers. See Rubia.

When the petals of the tulip become striped with many colours, the plant loses almost half of its height; and the method of making them thus break into colours is by transplanting them into a meagre or sandy soil, after they have previously enjoyed a richer soil: hence it appears, that the plant is weakened when the flower becomes variegated. See note on Anemone. For the acquired habits of vegetables, see Tulipa, Orchis.

The roots of the Arum are scratched up and eaten by thrushes in severe snowy seasons. White's Hist. of Selbourn, p. 43.]

> While Love's soft beams illume her treacherous eyes,
> And Beauty lightens through the thin disguise.
> 285 So erst, when HERCULES, untamed by toil,
> Own'd the soft power of DEJANIRA'S smile;—
> His lion-spoils the laughing Fair demands,
> And gives the distaff to his awkward hands;
> O'er her white neck the bristly mane she throws,
> 290 And binds the gaping whiskers on her brows;   290
> Plaits round her slender waist the shaggy vest,
> And clasps the velvet paws across her breast.
> Next with soft hands the knotted club she rears,
> Heaves up from earth, and on her shoulder bears.
> 295 Onward with loftier step the Beauty treads,   295
> And trails the brinded ermine o'er the meads;
> Wolves, bears, and pards, forsake the affrighted groves,
> And grinning Satyrs tremble, as she moves.
>
> CARYO'S sweet smile DIANTHUS proud admires,
> 300 And gazing burns with unallow'd desires;   300

[*Dianthus*. l. 299. Superbus. Proud Pink. There is a kind of pink called Fairchild's mule, which is here supposed to be produced between a Dianthus superbus, and the Garyophyllus, Clove. The Dianthus superbus emits a most fragrant odour, particularly at night. Vegetable mules supply an irrefragable argument in favour of the sexual system of botany. They are said to be numerous; and, like the mules of the animal kingdom, not always to continue their species by seed. There is an account of a curious mule from the Antirrbinum linaria, Toad-flax, in the Amoenit. Academ. V. I. No. 3. and many hybrid plants described in No. 32. The Urtica alienata is an evergreen plant, which appears to be a nettle from the male flowers, and a Pellitory (Parietaria) from the female ones and the fruit; and is hence between both. Murray, Syft. Veg. Amongst the English indigenous plants, the veronica hybrida mule Speedwel is supposed to have originated from the officinal one; and the spiked one, and the Sibthorpia Europæa to have for its parents the golden saxifrage and marsh pennywort. Pulteney's View of Linneus, p. 250. Mr. Graberg, Mr. Schreber, and Mr. Ramstrom, seem of opinion, that the internal structure or parts of fructification in mule-plants resemble the female parent; but that the habit or external structure resembles the male parent. See treatises under the above names in V. VI. Amænit. Academic. The mule produced from a horse and the ass resembles the horse externally with his ears, main, and tail; but with the nature or manners of an ass: but the Hinnus, or creature produced from a male ass, and a mare, resembles the father externally in stature, ash-colour, and the black cross, but with the nature or manners of a horse. The breed from Spanish rams and Swedish ewes resembled the Spanish sheep in wool, stature, and external form; but was as hardy as the Swedish sheep; and the contrary of those which were produced from Swedish rams and Spanish ewes. The offspring from the male goat of Angora and the Swedish female goat had long soft camel's hair; but that from the male Swedish goat, and the female one of Angora, had no improvement of their wool. An English ram without horns, and a Swedish horned ewe, produced sheep without horns. Amoen. Academ. V. VI. p. 13.]

With sighs and sorrows her compassion moves,
And wins the damsel to illicit loves.
The Monster-offspring heirs the father's pride,
Mask'd in the damask beauties of the bride.
305 So, when the Nightingale in eastern bowers
On quivering pinion woos the Queen of flowers;
Inhales her fragrance, as he hangs in air,
And melts with melody the blushing fair;
Half-rose, half-bird, a beauteous Monster springs,
310 Waves his thin leaves, and claps his glossy wings;
Long horrent thorns his mossy legs surround,
And tendril-talons root him to the ground;
Green films of rind his wrinkled neck o'espread,
And crimson petals crest his curled head;
315 Soft-warbling beaks in each bright blossom move,
And vocal Rosebuds thrill the enchanted grove!—
Admiring Evening stays her beamy star,
And still Night listens from his ebon car;
While on white wings descending Houries throng,
320 And drink the floods of odour and of song.

When from his golden urn the Solstice pours
O'er Afric's sable sons the sultry hours;

When not a gale flits o'er her tawny hills,
Save where the dry Harmattan breathes and kills;

[*The dry Harmattan.* l. 324. The Harmattan is a singular wind blowing from the interior parts of Africa to the Atlantic ocean, sometimes for a few hours, sometimes for several days without regular periods. It is always attended with a fog or haze, so dense as to render those objects invisible which are at the distance of a quarter of a mile; the sun appears through it only about noon, and then of a dilute red, and very minute particles subside from the misty air so as to make the grass, and the skins of negroes appear whitish. The extreme dryness which attends this wind or fog, without dews, withers and quite dries the leaves of vegetables; and is said of Dr. Lind at some seasons to be fatal and malignant to mankind; probably after much preceding wet, when it may become loaded with the exhalations from putrid marshes; at other seasons it is said to check epidemic diseases, to cure fluxes, and to heal ulcers and cutaneous eruptions; which is probably effected by its yielding no moisture to the mouths of the external absorbent vessels, by which the action of the other branches of the absorbent system is increased to supply the deficiency. *Account of the Harmattan. Phil. Transact. V. LXXI.*

The Rev. Mr. Sterling gives an account of a darkness for six or eight hours at Detroit in America, on the 19th of October, 1762, in which the sun appeared as red as blood, and thrice its usual size: some rain falling, covered white paper with dark drops, like sulphur or dirt, which burnt like wet gunpowder, and the air had a very sulphureous smell. He supposes this to have been emitted from some distant earthquake or volcano. Philos. Trans. V. LIII. p. 63.

In many circumstances this wind seems much to resemble the dry fog which covered most parts of Europe for many weeks in the summer of 1780, which has been supposed to have had a volcanic origin, as it succeeded the violent eruption of Mount Hecla, and its neighbourhood. From the subsidence of a white powder, it seems probable that the Harmattan has a similar origin, from the unexplored mountains of Africa. Nor is it improbable, that the epidemic coughs, which occasionally traverse immense tracts of country, may be the products of volcanic eruptions; nor impossible, that at some future time contagious miasmata may be thus emitted from subterraneous furnaces, in such abundance as to contaminate the whole atmosphere, and depopulate the earth!]

325 When stretch'd in dust her gasping panthers lie,
And writh'd in foamy folds her serpents die;
Indignant Atlas mourns his leafless woods,
And Gambia trembles for his sinking floods;
Contagion stalks along the briny sand,
330 And Ocean rolls his sickening shoals to land.

[*His sickening shoals.* 330. Mr. Marsden relates, that in the island of Sumatra, during the November of 1775, the dry monsoons, or S.E. winds, continued so much longer than usual, that the large rivers became dry; and prodigious quantities of sea-fish, dead and dying, were seen floating for leagues on the sea, and driven on the beach by the tides. This was supposed to have been caused by the great evaporation, and the deficiency of fresh water rivers having rendered the sea too fast for its inhabitants. The season then became so sickly as to destroy great numbers of people, both foreigners and natives. Phil. Trans. V. LXXI. p. 384.]

—Fair CHUNDA smiles amid the burning waste,
Her brow unturban'd, and her zone unbrac'd;
Ten brother-youths with light umbrella's shade,
Or fan with busy hands the panting maid;
335 Loose wave her locks, disclosing, as they break,
The rising bosom and averted cheek;

[*Chunda*. l. 331. *Chundali Borrum* is the name which the natives give to this plant; it is the Hedylarum gyrans, or moving plant; its class is two brotherhoods, ten males. Its leaves are continually in spontaneous motion; some rising and others falling; and others whirling circularly by twisting their stems; this spontaneous movement of the leaves, when the air is quite still and very warm, seems to be necessary to the plant, at perpetual respiration is to animal life. A more particular account, with a good print of the Hedyfarum gyrans is given by M. Brouffonet in a paper on vegetable motions in the Histoire de l'Academie des Sciences. Ann. 1784, p. 609.

There are many other instances of spontaneous movements of the parts of vegetables. In the Marchantia polymorpha some yellow wool proceeds from the flower-bearing anthers, which moves spontaneously in the anther, while it drops its dust like atoms. Murray, Syst. Veg. See note on Collinfonia for other instances of vegetable spontaneity. Add to this, that as the sleep of animals consists in a suspension of voluntary motion, and as vegetables are likewise subject to sleep, there is reason to conclude, that the various actions of opening and closing their petals and foliage may be justly ascribed to a voluntary power: for without the faculty of volition, sleep would not have been, necessary to them.]

Clasp'd round her ivory neck with studs of gold
Flows her thin vest in many a gauzy fold;
O'er her light limbs the dim transparence plays,
340 And the fair form, it seems to hide, betrays.

Where leads the northern Star his lucid train
High o'er the snow-clad earth, and icy main,
With milky light the white horizon streams,
And to the moon each sparkling mountain gleams.—
345 Slow o'er the printed snows with silent walk

Huge shaggy forms across the twilight stalk;
And ever and anon with hideous sound
Burst the thick ribs of ice, and thunder round.—
There, as old Winter flaps his hoary wing,
350 And lingering leaves his empire to the Spring,
Pierced with quick shafts of silver-shooting light
Fly in dark troops the dazzled imps of night—

[*Burst the thick rib of ice.* l. 348. The violent cracks of ice heard from the Glaciers seem to be caused by some of the snow being melted in the middle of the day; and the water thus produced running down into vallies of ice, and congealing again in a few hours, forces off by its expansion large precipices from the ice-mountains.]

"Awake, my Love!" enamour'd MUSCHUS cries,
"Stretch thy fair limbs, refulgent Maid! arise;
355 Ope thy sweet eye-lids to the rising ray,
And hail with ruby lips returning day.
Down the white hills dissolving torrents pour,
Green springs the turf, and purple blows the flower;
His torpid wing the Rail exulting tries,
360 Mounts the soft gale, and wantons in the skies;
Rise, let us mark how bloom the awaken'd groves,
And 'mid the banks of roses *hide* our loves."

[*Muschus.* l. 353. Corallinus, or lichen rangiferinus. Coral-moss. Clandestine-marriage. This moss vegetates beneath the snow, where the degree of heat is always about 40; that is, in the middle between the freezing point, and the common heat of the earth; and is for many months of the winter the sole food of the rain-deer, who digs furrows in the snow to find it: and as the milk and flesh of this animal is almost the only sustenance which can be procured during the long winters of the higher latitudes, this moss may be said to support some millions of mankind.

The quick vegetation that occurs on the solution of the snows in high latitudes appears very astonishing; it seems to arise from two causes, 1. the long continuance of the approaching sun above the horizon; 2. the increased irritability of plants which have been long exposed to the cold. See note on Anemone.

All the water-fowl on the lakes of Siberia are said by Professor Gmelin to retreat Southwards on the commencement of the frosts, except the Rail, which sleeps buried in the snow. Account of Siberia.]

Night's tinsel beams on smooth Lock-lomond dance,
Impatient ÆGA views the bright expanse;—
365 In vain her eyes the parting floods explore,

Wave after wave rolls freightless to the shore.
—Now dim amid the distant foam she spies
A rising speck,—"'tis he! 'tis he!" She cries;
As with firm arms he beats the streams aside,
370 And cleaves with rising chest the tossing tide,
With bended knee she prints the humid sands,
Up-turns her glistening eyes, and spreads her hands;
—"'Tis he, 'tis he!—My Lord, my life, my love!—
Slumber, ye winds; ye billows, cease to move!
375 Beneath his arms your buoyant plumage spread,
Ye Swans! ye Halcyons! hover round his head!"—

[*Æga* l. 364. Conserva ægagropila. It is found loose in many lakes in a globular form, from the size of a walnut to that of a melon, much resembling the balls of hair found in the stomachs of cows; it adheres to nothing, but rolls from one part of the lake to another. The Conserva vagabunda dwells on the European seas, travelling along in the midst of the waves; (Spec. Plant.) These may not improperly be called itinerant vegetables. In a similar manner the Fucus natans (swimming) strikes no roots into the earth, but floats on the sea in very extensive masses, and may be said to be a plant of passage, as it is wafted by the winds from one shore to another.]

—With eager step the boiling surf she braves,
And meets her refluent lover in the waves;
Loose o'er the flood her azure mantle swims,
380 And the clear stream betrays her snowy limbs.

So on her sea-girt tower fair HERO stood
At parting day, and mark'd the dashing flood;
While high in air, the glimmering rocks above,
Shone the bright lamp, the pilot-star of Love.
385 —With robe outspread the wavering flame behind
She kneels, and guards it from the shifting wind;
Breathes to her Goddess all her vows, and guides
Her bold LEANDER o'er the dusky tides;
Wrings his wet hair, his briny bosom warms,
390 And clasps her panting lover in her arms.

Deep, in wide caverns and their shadowy ailes,
Daughter of Earth, the chaste TRUFFELIA smiles;

[*Truffelia.* l. 392. (Lycoperdon Tuber) Truffle. Clandestine marriage. This fungus never appears above ground, requiring little air, and perhaps no light. It is found by dogs or swine, who hunt it by the smell. Other plants, which have no buds or branches on their stems, as the grasses, shoot out numerous stoles or scions underground; and this the more, as their tops or herbs are eaten by cattle, and thus preserve themselves,]

On silvery beds, of soft asbestus wove,
Meets her Gnome-husband, and avows her love.
395 —*High* o'er her couch impending diamonds blaze,
And branching gold the crystal roof inlays;
With verdant light the modest emeralds glow,
Blue sapphires glare, and rubies blush, *below*;
Light piers of lazuli the dome surround,
400 And pictured mochoes tesselate the ground;
In glittering threads along reflective walls
The warm rill murmuring twinkles, as it falls;
Now sink the Eolian strings, and now they swell,
And Echoes woo in every vaulted cell;
405 While on white wings delighted Cupids play,
Shake their bright lamps, and shed celestial day.

Closed in an azure fig by fairy spells,
Bosom'd in down, fair CAPRI-FICA dwells;—

[*Caprificus*. l. 408 Wild fig. The fruit of the fig is not a seed-vessel, but a receptacle inclosing the flower within it. As these trees bear some male and others female flowers, immured on all sides by the fruit, the manner of their fecundation was very unintelligible, till Tournefort and Pontedera discovered, that a kind of gnat produced in the male figs carried the fecundating dust on its wings, (Cynips Psenes Syst. Nat. 919.), and, penetrating the female fig, thus impregnated the flowers; for the evidence of this wonderful fact, see the word Caprification, in Milne's Botanical Dictionary. The figs of this country are all female, and their seeds not prolific; and therefore they can only be propagated by layers and suckers.

Monsieur de la Hire has shewn in the Memoir, de l'Academ. de Science, that the summer figs of Paris, in Provence, Italy, and Malta, have all perfect stamina, and ripen not only their fruits, but their seed; from which seed other fig-trees are raised; but that the stamina of the autumnal figs are abortive, perhaps owing to the want of due warmth. Mr. Milne, in his Botanical Dictionary (art. Caprification), says, that the cultivated fig-trees have a few male flowers placed above the female within the same covering or receptacle; which in warmer climates perform their proper office, but in colder ones become abortive: And Linneus observes, that some figs have the navel of the receptacle open; which was one reason that induced him to remove this plant from the class Clandestine Marriage to the class Polygamy. Lin. Spec. Plant.

From all these circumstances I should conjecture, that those female fig-flowers, which are closed on all sides in the fruit or receptacle without any male ones, are monsters, which have been propagated for their fruit, like barberries, and grapes without seeds in them; and that the Caprification is either an ancient process of imaginary use, and blindly followed in some countries, or that it may contribute to ripen the fig by decreasing its vigour, like cutting off a circle of the bark from the branch of a pear-tree. Tournefort seems inclined to this opinion; who says, that the figs in Provence and at Paris ripen sooner, if their buds be pricked with a straw dipped in olive-oil. Plumbs and pears punctured by some insects ripen sooner, and the part round the puncture is sweeter. Is not the honey-dew produced by the puncture of insects? will not wounding the branch of a pear-tree, which is too vigorous, prevent the blossoms from falling off; as from some fig-trees the fruit is said to fall off unless they are wounded by caprification? I had last spring six young trees of the Ischia fig with fruit on them in pots in a stove; on removing them into larger boxes, they protruded very vigorous shoots, and the figs all fell off; which I ascribed to the increased vigour of the plants.]

    So sleeps in silence the Curculio, shut
410 In the dark chambers of the cavern'd nut,
     Erodes with ivory beak the vaulted shell,
     And quits on filmy wings its narrow cell.
     So the pleased Linnet in the moss-wove nest,
     Waked into life beneath its parent's breast,
415 Chirps in the gaping shell, bursts forth erelong,
     Shakes its new plumes, and tries its tender song.—
     —And now the talisman she strikes, that charms
     Her husband-Sylph,—and calls him to her arms.—
     Quick, the light Gnat her airy Lord bestrides,
420 With cobweb reins the flying courser guides,
     From crystal steeps of viewless ether springs,
     Cleaves the soft air on still expanded wings;
     Darts like a sunbeam o'er the boundless wave,
     And seeks the beauty in her *secret* cave.
425 So with quick impulse through all nature's frame
     Shoots the electric air its subtle flame.
     So turns the impatient needle to the pole,
     Tho' mountains rise between, and oceans roll.
     Where round the Orcades white torrents roar,
430 Scooping with ceaseless rage the incumbent shore,
     Wide o'er the deep a dusky cavern bends
     Its marble arms, and high in air impends;
     Basaltic piers the ponderous roof sustain,
     And steep their massy sandals in the main;
435 Round the dim walls, and through the whispering ailes
     Hoarse breathes the wind, the glittering water boils.
     Here the charm'd BYSSUS with his blooming bride
     Spreads his green sails, and braves the foaming tide;

The star of Venus gilds the twilight wave,
440 And lights her votaries to the *secret* cave;
Light Cupids flutter round the nuptial bed,
And each coy sea-maid hides her blushing head.

[*Basaltic piers.* l. 433. This description alludes to the cave of Fingal in the island of Staffa. The basaltic columns, which compose the Giants Causeway on the coast of Ireland, as well as those which support the cave of Fingal, are evidently of volcanic origin, as is well illustrated in an ingenious paper of Mr. Keir, in the Philos. Trans. who observed in the glass, which had been long in a fusing heat at the bottom of the pots in the glass-houses at Stourbridge, that crystals were produced of a form similar to the parts of the basaltic columns of the Giants Causeway.]

[*Byssus.* 437. Clandestine Marriage. It floats on the sea in the day, and sinks a little during the night; it is found in caverns on the northern shores, of a pale green colour, and as thin as paper.]

Where cool'd by rills, and curtain'd round by woods,
Slopes the green dell to meet the briny floods,
445 The sparkling noon-beams trembling on the tide,
The PROTEUS-LOVER woos his playful bride,
To win the fair he tries a thousand forms,
Basks on the sands, or gambols in the storms.
A Dolphin now, his scaly sides he laves,
450 And bears the sportive damsel on the waves;
She strikes the cymbal as he moves along,
And wondering Ocean listens to the song.
—And now a spotted Pard the lover stalks,
Plays round her steps, and guards her favour'd walks;

[*The Proteus-love.* l. 446. Conserva polymorpha. This vegetable is put amongst the cryptogamia, or clandestine marriages, by Linneus; but, according to Mr. Ellis, the males and females are on different plants. Philos. Trans. Vol. LVII. It twice changes its colour, from red to brown, and then to black; and changes its form by losing its lower leaves, and elongating some of the upper ones, so as to be mistaken by the unskilful for different plants. It grows on the shores of this country.

There is another plant, Medicago polymorpha, which may be said to assume a great variety of shapes; as the seed-vessels resemble sometimes snail-horns, at other times caterpillars with or without long hair upon them; by which means it is probable they sometimes elude the depredations of those insects. The seeds of Calendula, Marygold, bend up like a hairy caterpillar, with their prickles bridling outwards, and may thus deter some birds or insects from preying upon them. Salicornia also assumes an animal similitude. Phil. Bot. p. 87. See note on Iris in additional notes; and Cypripedia in Vol. I.]

455 As with white teeth he prints her hand, caress'd,
  And lays his velvet paw upon her breast,
  O'er his round face her snowy fingers strain
  The silken knots, and fit the ribbon-rein.
  —And now a Swan, he spreads his plumy sails,
460 And proudly glides before the fanning gales;
  Pleas'd on the flowery brink with graceful hand
  She waves her floating lover to the land;
  Bright shines his sinuous neck, with crimson beak
  He prints fond kisses on her glowing cheek,
465 Spreads his broad wings, elates his ebon crest,
  And clasps the beauty to his downy breast.

  A *hundred* virgins join a *hundred* swains,
  And fond ADONIS leads the sprightly trains;

[*Adonis*. l. 468. Many males and many females live together in the same flower. It may seem a solecism in language, to call a flower, which contains many of both sexes, an individual; and the more so to call a tree or shrub an individual, which consists of so many flowers. Every tree, indeed, ought to be considered as a family or swarm of its respective buds; but the buds themselves seem to be individual plants; because each has leaves or lungs appropriated to it; and the bark of the tree is only a congeries of the roots of all these individual buds. Thus hollow oak-trees and willows are often seen with the whole wood decayed and gone; and yet the few remaining branches flourish with vigour; but in respect to the male and female parts of a flower, they do not destroy its individuality any more than the number of paps of a sow, or the number of her cotyledons, each of which includes one of her young.

The society, called the Areoi, in the island of Otaheite, consists of about 100 males and 100 females, who form one promiscuous marriage.]

  Pair after pair, along his sacred groves
470 To Hymen's fane the bright procession moves;
  Each smiling youth a myrtle garland shades,
  And wreaths of roses veil the blushing maids;
  Light joys on twinkling feet attend the throng,
  Weave the gay dance, or raise the frolic song;
475 —Thick, as they pass, exulting Cupids fling
  Promiscuous arrows from the sounding string;
  On wings of gossamer soft Whispers fly,
  And the sly Glance steals side-long from the eye.
  —As round his shrine the gaudy circles bow,
480 And seal with muttering lips the faithless vow,
  Licentious Hymen joins their mingled hands,

attractive but no value or integrity

And loosely twines the meretricious bands.—
Thus where pleased VENUS, in the southern main,
Sheds all her smiles on Otaheite's plain,

485 Wide o'er the isle her silken net she draws,
And the Loves laugh at all, but Nature's laws."
Here ceased the Goddess,—o'er the silent strings
Applauding Zephyrs swept their fluttering wings;
Enraptur'd Sylphs arose in murmuring crowds
490 To air-wove canopies and pillowy clouds;
Each Gnome reluctant sought his earthy cell,
And each bright Floret clos'd her velvet bell.
Then, on soft tiptoe, NIGHT approaching near
Hung o'er the tuneless lyre his sable ear;
495 Gem'd with bright stars the still etherial plain,
And bad his Nightingales repeat the strain.

ADDITIONAL NOTES:

P. 7. *Additional note to Curcuma.* These anther-less filaments seem to be an endeavour of the plant to produce more stamens, as would appear from some experiments of M. Reynier, instituted for another purpose: he cut away the stamens of many flowers, with design to prevent their fecundity, and in many instances the flower threw out new filaments from the wounded part of different lengths; but did not produce new anthers. The experiments were made on the geum rivale, different kinds of mallows, and the æchinops ritro. Critical Review for March, 1788.

P. 8. *Addition to the note on Iris.* In the Persian Iris the end of the lower petal is purple, with white edges and orange streaks, creeping, as it were, into the mouth of the flower like an insect; by which deception in its native climate it probably prevents a similar insect from plundering it of its honey: the edges of the lower petal lap over those of the upper one, which prevents it from opening too wide on fine days, and facilitates its return at night; whence the rain is excluded, and the air admitted. See Polymorpha, Rubia, and Cypripedia in Vol. I.

P. 12. *Additional note on Chandrilla.* In the natural state of the expanded flower of the barberry, the stamens lie on the petals; under the concave summits of which the anthers shelter themselves, and in this situation remain perfectly rigid; but on touching the inside of the filament near its base with a fine bristle, or blunt needle, the stamen instantly bends upwards, and the anther, embracing the stigma, sheds its dust. Observations on the Irritation of Vegetables, by T. E. Smith, M. D.

P. 15. *Addition to the note on Silene.* I saw a plant of the Dionaea Muscipula, Flytrap of Venus, this day, in the collection of Mr. Boothby at Ashbourn-Hall, Derbyshire, Aug. 20th, 1788; and on drawing a straw along the middle of the rib of the leaves as they lay upon the ground round the stem, each of them, in about a second of time, closed and doubled itself up, crossing the thorns over the opposite edge of the leaf, like the teeth of a spring rap-trap: of this plant I was favoured with an elegant coloured drawing, by Miss Maria Jackson of Tarporly, in Cheshire, a Lady who adds much botanical knowledge to many other elegant acquirements. In the Apocynum Androsaemifolium, one kind of Dog's bane, the anthers converge over the nectaries, which consist of five glandular oval corpuscles surrounding the germ; and at the same time admit air to the nectaries at the interstice between each anther. But when a fly inserts its proboscis between these anthers to plunder the honey, they converge closer, and with such violence as to detain the fly, which thus generally perishes. This account was related to me by R.W. Darwin, Esq; of Elston, in Nottinghamshire, who showed me the plant in flower, July 2d, 1788, with a fly thus held fast by the end of its proboscis, and was well seen by a magnifying lens, and which in vain repeatedly struggled to disengage itself, till the converging anthers were separated by means of a pin: on some days he had observed that almost every flower of this elegant plant had a fly in it thus entangled; and a few weeks afterwards favoured me with his further observations on this subject.

"My Apocynum is not yet out of flower. I have often visited it, and have frequently found four or five flies, some alive, and some dead, in its flowers; they are generally caught by the trunk or proboscis, sometimes by the trunk and a leg; there is one at present only caught by a leg: I don't know that this plant sleeps, as the flowers remain open in the night; yet the flies frequently make their escape. In a plant of Mr. Ordino's, an ingenious gardener at Newark, who is possessed of a great collection of plants, I saw many flowers of an Apocynum with three dead flies in each; they are a thin-bodied fly, and rather less than the common house-fly; but I have seen two or three other sorts of flies thus arrested by the plant. Aug. 12, 1788."

P. 18. *Additional note on Ilex.* The efficient cause which renders the hollies prickly in Needwood Forest only as high as the animals can reach them, may arise from the lower branches being constantly cropped by them, and thus shoot forth more luxuriant foliage: it is probable the shears in garden-hollies may produce the same effect, which is equally curious, as prickles are not thus produced on other plants.

P. 41. *Additional note on Ulva.* M. Hubert made some observations on the air contained in the cavities of the bambou. The stems of these canes were from 40 to 50 feet in height, and 4 or 5 inches in diameter, and might contain about 30 pints of elastic air. He cut a bambou, and introduced a lighted candle into the cavity, which was extinguished immediately on its entrance. He tried this about 60 times in a cavity of the bambou, containing about two pints. He introduced mice at different times into these cavities, which seemed to be somewhat affected, but soon recovered their agility. The stem of the bambou is not hollow till it rises more than one foot from the earth; the divisions between the cavities are convex downwards. Observ. sur la Physique par M. Rozier, l. 33. p. 130.

P. 65. *Additional note on Gossypium.*

———emerging Naïads cull
From leathery pods the vegetable wool.
———*eam circum Milesia vellera nymphæ*
Carpebant, hyali saturo fucata colore.

Virg. Georg. IV. 334.

P. 119. *Addition to Orchis.* The two following lines were by mistake omitted; they were to have been inserted after l. 282, p. 119.

Saw on his helm, her virgin hands inwove,
Bright stars of gold, and mystic knots of love;

P. 136. *Addition to the note on Tropæolum.* In Sweden a very curious phenomenon has been observed on certain flowers, by M. Haggren, Lecturer in Natural History. One evening be perceived a faint flash of light repeatedly dart from a Marigold; surprized at such an uncommon appearance, he resolved to examine it with attention; and, to be assured that it was no deception of the eye, he placed a man near him, with orders to make a signal at the moment when he observed the light. They both saw it constantly at the same moment.

The light was most brilliant on Marigolds, of an orange or flame colour; but scarcely visible on pale ones.

The flash was frequently seen on the same flower two or three times in quick succession, but more commonly at intervals of several minutes; and when several flowers in the same place emitted their light together, it could be observed at a considerable distance.

This phaenomenon was remarked in the months of July and August, at sun-set, and for half an hour after, when the atmosphere was clear; but after a rainy day, or when the air was loaded with vapours, nothing of it was seen.

The following flowers emitted flashes, more or less vivid, in this order:

1. The Marigold, *(Calendula Officinalis).*
2. Garden Nasturtion, *(Tropæolum majus).*
3. Orange Lily, *(Lilium bulbiferum).*
4. The Indian Pink, *(Tagetes patula et erecta).*

Sometimes it was also observed on the Sun-flowers, *(Helianthus annuus).* But bright yellow, or flame colour, seemed in general necessary for the production of this light; for it was never seen on the flowers of any other colour.

To discover whether some little insects, or phosphoric worms, might not be the cause of it, the flowers were carefully examined even with a microscope, without any such being found.

From the rapidity of the flash, and other circumstances, it might be conjectured, that there is something of electricity in this phaenomenon. It is well known, that when the *pistil* of a flower is impregnated, the *pollen* bursts away by its elasticity, with which electricity may be combined. But M. Haggren, after having observed the slash from the Orange-lily, the *anthers* of which are a considerable space distant from the *petals,* found that the light proceeded from the *petals* only; whence he concludes, that this electric light is caused by the *pollen,* which in flying off is scattered upon the *petals.* Obser. Physique par M. Rozier, Vol. XXXIII. p. iii.

P. 153. *Addition to Avena.* The following lines were by mistake omitted; they were designed to have been inserted after l. 102, p. 153.

> Green swells the beech, the widening knots improve,
> So spread the tender growths of culture'd love;
> Wave follows wave, the letter'd lines decay,

So Love's soft forms neglected melt away.

P. 157. *Additional note to Bellis.* Du Halde gives an account of a white wax made by small insects round the branches of a tree in China in great quantity, which is there collected for economical and medical purposes: the tree is called Tong-tsin. Description of China, Vol. I. p. 230.

Description of the Poison-Tree in the Island of JAVA. Translated from the original Dutch of N. P. Foerich.

This destructive tree is called in the Malayan language *Bohon-Upas,* and has been described by naturalists; but their accounts have been so tinctured with the *marvellous,* that the whole narration has been supposed to be an ingenious fiction by the generality of readers. Nor is this in the least degree surprising, when the circumstances which we shall faithfully relate in this description are considered.

I must acknowledge, that I long doubted the existence of this tree, until a stricter enquiry convinced me of my error. I shall now only relate simple unadorned facts, of which I have been an eye-witness. My readers may depend upon the fidelity of this account. In the year 1774 I was stationed at Batavia, as surgeon, in the service of the Dutch East-India Company. During my residence there I received several different accounts of the Bohon Upas, and the violent effects of its poison. They all then seemed incredible to me, but raised my curiosity in so high a degree, that I resolved to investigate this subject thoroughly, and to trust only to *my own observations.* In consequence of this resolution, I applied to the Governor-General, Mr. Petrus Albertus van der Parra, for a pass to travel through the country: my request was granted; and, having procured every information. I set out on my expedition. I had procured a recommendation from an old Malayan priest to another priest, who lives on the nearest inhabitable spot to the tree, which is about fifteen or sixteen miles distant. The letter proved of great service to me in my undertaking, as that priest is appointed by the Emperor to reside there, in order to prepare for eternity the souls of those who for different crimes are sentenced to approach the tree, and to procure the poison.

The *Bohon-Upas* is situated in the island of *Java,* about twenty-seven leagues from *Batavia,* fourteen from *Soura Charta,* the seat of the Emperor, and between eighteen and twenty leagues from *Tinksor,* the present residence of the Sultan of Java. It is surrounded on all sides by a circle of high hills and mountains; and the country round it, to the distance of ten or twelve miles from the tree, is entirely barren. Not a tree, nor a shrub, nor even the least plant or grass is to be seen. I have made the tour all around this dangerous spot, at about eighteen miles distant from the centre, and I found the aspect of the country on all sides equally dreary. The easiest ascent of the hills is from that part where the old ecclesiastick dwells. From his house the criminals are sent for the poison, into which the points of all warlike instruments are dipped. It is of high value, and produces a considerable revenue to the Emperor.

Account of the manner in which the Poison it procured.

The poison which is procured from this tree is a gum that issues out between the bark and the tree itself, like the *camphor*. Malefactors, who for their crimes are sentenced to die, are the only persons who fetch the poison; and this is the only chance they have of saving their lives. After sentence is pronounced upon them by the judge, they are asked in court, whether they will die by the hands of the executioner, or whether they will go to the Upas tree for a box of poison? They commonly prefer the latter proposal, as there is not only some chance of preserving their lives, but also a certainty, in case of their safe return, that a provision will be made for them in future by the Emperor. They are also permitted to ask a favour from the Emperor, which is generally of a trifling nature, and commonly granted. They are then provided with a silver or tortoiseshell box, in which they are to put the poisonous gum, and are properly instructed how to proceed while they are upon their dangerous expedition. Among other particulars, they are always told to attend to the direction of the winds; as they are to go towards the tree before the wind, so that the effluvia from the tree are always blown from them. They are told, likewise, to travel with the utmost dispatch, as that is the only method of insuring a safe return. They are afterwards sent to the house of the old priest, to which place they are commonly attended by their friends and relations. Here they generally remain some days, in expectation of a favourable breeze. During that time the ecclesiastic prepares them for their future fate by prayers and admonitions. When the hour of their departure arrives, the priest puts them on a long leather-cap, with two glasses before their eyes, which comes down as far as their breast; and also provides them with a pair of leather-gloves. They are then conducted by the priest, and their friends and relations, about two miles on their journey. Here the priest repeats his instructions, and tells them where they are to look for the tree. He shews them a hill, which they are told to ascend, and that on the other side they will find a rivulet, which they are to follow, and which will conduct them directly to the Upas. They now take leave of each other; and, amidst prayers for their success, the delinquents hasten away. The worthy old ecclesiastic has assured me, that during his residence there, for upwards of thirty years, he had dismissed above seven hundred criminals in the manner which I have described; and that scarcely two out of twenty have returned. He shewed me a catalogue of all the unhappy sufferers, with the date of their departure from his house annexed; and a list of the offences for which they had been condemned: to which was added, a list of those who had returned in safety. I afterwards saw another list of these culprits, at the jail keeper's at *Soura-Charta*, and found that they perfectly corresponded with each other, and with the different informations which I afterwards obtained. I was present at some of these melancholy ceremonies, and desired different delinquents to bring with them some pieces of the wood, or a small branch, or some leaves of this wonderful tree. I have also given them silk cords, desiring them to measure its thickness. I never could procure move than two dry leaves that were picked up by one of them on his return; and all I could learn from him, concerning the tree itself, was, that it stood on the border of a rivulet, as described by the old priest; that it was of a middling size; that five or six young trees of the same kind stood close by it; but that no other shrub or plant could be seen near it; and that the ground was of a brownish sand, full of stones, almost impracticable for travelling, and covered with dead bodies. After many conversations with the old Malayan priest, I questioned him about the first discovery, and asked his opinion of this dangerous tree; upon which he gave me the following answer:

"We are told in our new Alcoran, that, above an hundred years ago, the country around the tree was inhabited by a people strongly addicted to the sins of Sodom and Gomorrha; when the great prophet Mahomet determined not to suffer them to lead such detestable lives any longer, he applied to God to punish them: upon which God caused this tree to grow out of the earth, which destroyed them all, and rendered the country for ever uninhabitable."

Such was the Malayan opinion. I shall not attempt a comment; but must observe, that all the Malayans consider this tree as an holy instrument of the great prophet to punish the sins of mankind; and, therefore, to die of the poison of the Upas is generally considered among them as an honourable death. For that reason I also observed, that the delinquents, who were going to the tree, were generally dressed in their best apparel.

This however is certain, though it may appear incredible, that from fifteen to eighteen miles round this tree, not only no human creature can exist, but that, in that space of ground, no living animal of any kind has ever been discovered. I have also been assured by several persons of veracity, that there are no fish in the waters, nor has any rat, mouse, or any other vermin, been seen there; and when any birds fly so near this tree that the effluvia reaches them, they fall a sacrifice to the effects of the poison. This circumstance has been ascertained by different delinquents, who, in their return, have seen the birds drop down, and have picked them up *dead,* and brought them to the old ecclesiastick.

I will here mention an instance, which proves them a fact beyond all doubt, and which happened during my stay at Java.

In the year 1775 a rebellion broke out among the subjects of the Massay, a sovereign prince, whose dignity is nearly equal to that of the Emperor. They refused to pay a duty imposed upon them by their sovereign, whom they openly opposed. The Massay sent a body of a thousand troops to disperse the rebels, and to drive them, with their families, out of his dominions. Thus four hundred families, consisting of above sixteen hundred souls, were obliged to leave their native country. Neither the Emperor nor the Sultan would give them protection, not only because they were rebels, but also through fear of displeasing their neighbour, the Massay. In this distressful situation, they had no other resource than to repair to the uncultivated parts round the Upas, and requested permission of the Emperor to settle there. Their request was granted, on condition of their fixing their abode not more than twelve or fourteen miles from the tree, in order not to deprive the inhabitants already settled there at a greater distance of their cultivated lands. With this they were obliged to comply; but the consequence was, that in less than two months their number was reduced to about three hundred. The chiefs of those who remained returned to the Massay, informed him of their losses, and intreated his pardon, which induced him to receive them again as subjects, thinking them sufficiently punished for their misconduct. I have seen and conversed with several of those who survived soon after their return. They all had the appearance of persons tainted with an infectious disorder; they looked pale and weak, and from the account which they gave of the loss of their comrades, of the symptoms and circumstances which attended their dissolution, such as convulsions, and other signs of a violent death, I was fully convinced that they fell victims to the poison.

This violent effect of the poison at so great a distance from the tree, certainly appears surprising, and almost incredible; and especially when we consider that it is possible for delinquents who approach the tree to return alive. My wonder, however, in a great measure, ceased, after I had made the following observations:

I have said before, that malefactors are instructed to go to the tree with the wind, and to return against the wind. When the wind continues to blow from the same quarter while the delinquent travels thirty, or six and thirty miles, if he be of a good constitution, he certainly survives. But what proves the most destructive is, that there is no dependence on the wind in that part of the world for any length of time.—There are no regular land-winds; and the sea-wind is not perceived there at all, the situation of the tree being at too great a distance, and surrounded by high mountains and uncultivated forests. Besides, the wind there never blows a fresh regular gale, but is commonly merely a current of light, soft breezes, which pass through the different openings of the adjoining mountains. It is also frequently difficult to determine from what part of the globe the wind really comes, as it is divided by various obstructions in its passage, which easily change the direction of the wind, and often totally destroy its effects.

I, therefore, impute the distant effects of the poison, in a great measure, to the constant gentle winds in those parts, which have not power enough to disperse the poisonous particles. If high winds are more frequent and durable there, they would certainly weaken very much, and even destroy the obnoxious effluvia of the poison; but without them, the air remains infested and pregnant with these poisonous vapours.

I am the more convinced of this, as the worthy ecclesiastick assured me, that a dead calm is always attended with the greatest danger, as there is a continual perspiration issuing from the tree, which is seen to rise and spread in the air, like the putrid steam of a marshy cavern.

Experiments made with the Gum of the UPAS TREE.

In the year 1776, in the month of February, I was present at the execution of thirteen of the Emperor's concubines, at *Soura-Charta*, who were convicted of infidelity to the Emperor's bed. It was in the forenoon, about eleven o'clock, when the fair criminals were led into an open space within the walls of the

Emperor's palace. There the judge passed sentence upon them, by which they are doomed to suffer death by a lancet poisoned with Upas. After this the Alcoran was presented to them, and they were, according to the law of their great prophet Mahomet, to acknowledge and to affirm by oath, that the charges brought against them, together with the sentence and their punishment, were fair and equitable. This they did, by laying their right hand upon the Alcoran, their left hands upon their breast, and their eyes lifted towards heaven; the judge then held the Alcoran to their lips, and they kissed it.

These ceremonies over, the executioner proceeded on his business in the following manner:—Thirteen posts, each about five feet high, had been previously erected. To these the delinquents were fastened, and their breasts stripped naked. In this situation they remained a short time in continual prayers, attended by several priests, until a signal was given by the judge to the executioner; on which the latter produced an instrument, much like the spring lancet used by farriers for bleeding horses. With this instrument, it being poisoned with the gum of the Upas, the unhappy wretches were lanced in the middle of their breasts, and the operation was performed upon them all in less than two minutes.

My astonishment was raised to the highest degree, when I beheld the sudden effects of that poison, for in about five minutes after they were lanced, they were taken with a *tremor*, attended with a *subsultus tendinum*, after which they died in the greatest agonies, crying out to God and Mahomet for mercy. In sixteen minutes by my watch, which I held in my hand, all the criminals were no more. Some hours after their death, I observed their bodies full of livid spots, much like those of the *Petechiæ*, their faces swelled, their colour changed to a kind of blue, their eyes looked yellow, &c. &c.

About a fortnight after this, I had an opportunity of seeing such another execution at Samarang. Seven Malayans were executed there with the same instrument, and in the same manner; and I found the operation of the poison, and the spots in their bodies exactly the same.

These circumstances made me desirous to try an experiment with some animals, in order to be convinced of the real effects of this poison; and as I had then two young puppies, I thought them the fittest objects for my purpose. I accordingly procured with great difficulty some grains of Upas. I dissolved half a grain of that gum in a small quantity of arrack, and dipped a lancet into it. With this poisoned instrument I made an incision in the lower muscular part of the belly in one of the puppies. Three minutes after it received the wound the animal began to cry out most piteously, and ran as fast as possible from one corner of the room to the other. So it continued during six minutes, when all its strength being exhausted, it fell upon the ground, was taken with convulsions, and died in the eleventh minute. I repeated this experiment with two other puppies, with a cat, and a fowl, and found the operation of the poison in all of them the same: none of these animals survived above thirteen minutes.

I thought it necessary to try also the effect of the poison given inwardly, which I did in the following manner. I dissolved a quarter of a grain of the gum in half an ounce of arrack, and made a dog of seven months old drink it. In seven minutes a retching ensued, and I observed, at the same time, that the animal was delirious, as it ran up and down the room, fell on the ground, and tumbled about; then it rose again, cried out very loud, and in about half an hour after was seized with convulsions, and died. I opened the body, and found the stomach very much inflamed, as the intestines were in some parts, but not so much as the stomach. There was a small quantity of coagulated blood in the stomach; but I could discover no orifice from which it could have issued; and therefore supposed it to have been squeezed out of the lungs, by the animal's straining while it was vomiting.

From these experiments I have been convinced that the gum of the Upas is the most dangerous and most violent of all vegetable poisons; and I am apt to believe that it greatly contributes to the unhealthiness of that island. Nor is this the only evil attending it: hundreds of the natives of Java, as well as Europeans, are yearly destroyed and treacherously murdered by that poison, either internally or externally. Every man of quality or fashion has his dagger or other arms poisoned with it; and in times of war the Malayans poison the springs and other waters with it; by this treacherous practice the Dutch suffered greatly during the last war, as it occasioned the loss of half their army. For this reason, they have ever since kept fish in the springs of which they drink the water; and sentinels are placed near them, who inspect the waters every hour, to see whether the fish are alive. If they march with an army or body of troops into an enemy's country, they always carry live fish with them, which they throw into the water some hours before they venture to drink it; by which means they have been able to prevent their total destruction.

This account, I flatter myself, will satisfy the curiosity of my readers, and the few facts which I have related will be considered as a certain proof of the exigence of this pernicious tree, and its penetrating effects.

If it be asked why we have not yet any more satisfactory accounts of this tree, I can only answer, that the object to most travellers to that part of the world consists more in commercial pursuits than in the study of Natural History and the advancement of Sciences. Besides, Java is so universally reputed an unhealthy island, that rich travellers seldom make any long stay in it; and others want money, and generally are too ignorant of the language to travel, in order to make enquiries. In future, those who visit this island will probably now be induced to make it an object of their researches, and will furnish us with a fuller description of this tree.

I will therefore only add, that there exists also a sort of Cajoe-Upat on the coast of Macassar, the poison of which operates nearly in the same manner, but is not half so violent or malignant as that of Java, and of which I shall likewise give a more circumstantial account in a description of that island.—*London Magazine*.

CATALOGUE OF THE POETIC EXHIBITION.

CANTO I.

Group of insects—Tender husband—Self-admirer—Rival lovers—Coquet—Platonic wife—Monster-husband—Rural happiness—Clandestine marriage—Sympathetic lovers—Ninon d'Enclos—Harlots—Giants—Mr. Wright's paintings—Thalestris Autumnal scene—Dervise procession—Lady in full dress—Lady on a precipice—Palace in the sea—Vegetable lamb—Whale—Sensibility—Mountain-scene by night—Lady drinking water—Lady and cauldron—Medea and Æson—Forlorn nymph Galatea on the sea—Lady frozen to a statue

CANTO II.

Air-balloon of Mongolfier—Arts of weaving and spinning—Arkwright's cotton mills—Invention of letters, figures and crotchets—Mrs. Delany's paper-garden—Mechanism of a watch, and design for its case—Time, hours, moments—Transformation of Nebuchadnazer—St. Anthony preaching to fish Sorceress—Miss Crew's drawing—Song to May—Frost scene—Discovery of the bark—Moses striking the rock—Dropsy—Mr. Howard and prisons

CANTO III.

Witch and imps in a church—Inspired Priestess—Fusseli's night-mare—Cave of Thor and subterranean Naïads—Medea and her children—Palmira weeping Group of wild creatures drinking—Poison tree of Java—Time and hours—Lady shot in battle—Wounded deer—Harlots—Laocoon and his sons—Drunkards and diseases—Prometheus and the vulture—Lady burying her child in the plague Moses concealed on the Nile—Slavery of the Africans—Weeping Muse

CANTO IV.

Maid of night Fairies—Electric lady—Shadrec, Meshec, and Abednego, in the fiery furnace—Shepherdesses—Song to Echo—Kingdom of China—Lady and distaff—Cupid spinning—Lady walking in snow—Children at play—Venus and Loves—Matlock Bath—Angel bathing—Mermaid and Nereids—Lady in salt—Lot's wife—Lady in regimentals—Dejanira in a lion's skin—Offspring from the marriage of the Rose and Nightingale—Parched deserts in Africa—Turkish lady in an undress—Ice-scene in Lapland—Lock-lomond by moon light—Hero and Leander—Gnome-husband and Palace under ground—Lady inclosed in a fig—Sylph-husband—Marine cave—Proteus-lover—Lady on a Dolphin—Lady bridling a Pard—Lady saluted by a Swan—Hymeneal procession—Night

CONTENTS OF THE NOTES.

Seeds of Canna used for prayer-beads

Stems and leaves of Callitriche so matted together, as they float on the water, as to bear a person walking on them

The female in Collinsonia approaches first to one of the males, and then to the other

Females in Nigella and Epilobium bend towards the males for some days, and then leave them

The stigma or head of the female in Spartium (common broom) is produced amongst the higher set of males; but when the keal-leaf opens, the pistil suddenly twists round like a French-horn, and places the stigma amidst the lower set of males

The two lower males in Ballota become mature before the two higher; and, when their dust is shed, turn outwards from the female

The plants of the class Two Powers with naked seeds are all aromatic

Of these Marum and Nepeta are delightful to cats

The filaments in Meadia, Borago, Cyclamen, Solanum, &c. shewn by reasoning_ to be the most unchangeable parts of those flowers

Rudiments of two hinder wings are seen in the class Diptera, or two-winged insects

Teats of male animals

Filaments without anthers in Curcuma, Linum, &c. and styles without stigmas in many plants, shew the advance of the works of nature towards greater perfection

Double flowers, or vegetable monsters, how produced

The calyx and lower series of petals not changed in double flowers

Dispersion of the dust in nettles and other plants

Cedar and Cypress unperishable

Anthoxanthum gives the fragrant scent to hay

Viviparous plants: the Aphis is viviparous in summer, and oviparous in autumn

Irritability of the stamen of the plants of the class Syngenesia, or Confederate males

Some of the males in Lychnis, and other flowers arrive sooner at their maturity

Males approach the female in Gloriosa, Fritillaria, and Kalmia

Contrivances to destroy insects in Silene, Dionæa muscipula, Arum muscivorum, Dypsacus, &c.

Some bell-flowers close at night; others hang the mouths downwards; others nod and turn from the wind; stamens bound down to the pistil in Amaryllis formofissima; pistil is crooked in Hemerocallis flava, yellow day-lily Thorns and prickles designed for the defence of the plant; tall Hollies have no prickles above the reach of cattle

Bird-lime from the bark of Hollies like elastic gum

Adansonia the largest tree known, its dimensions

Bulbous roots contain the embryon flower, seen by dissecting a tulip-root

Flowers of Colchicum and Hamamelis appear in autumn, and ripen their seed in the spring following

Sunflower turns to the sun by nutation, not by gyration

Dispersion of seeds

Drosera catches flies

Of the nectary, its structure to preserve the honey from insects

Curious proboscis of the Sphinx Convolvoli

Final cause of the resemblance of some flowers to insects, as the Bee-orchis

In some plants of the class Tetradynamia, or Four Powers, the two shorter stamens, when at maturity, rise as high as the others

Ice in the caves on Teneriff, which were formerly hollowed by volcanic fires

Some parasites do not injure trees, as Tillandsia and Epidendrum

Mosses growing on trees injure them

Marriages of plants necessary to be celebrated in the air

Insects with legs on their backs

Scarcity of grain in wet seasons

Tartarian lamb; use of down on vegetables; air, glass, wax, and fat, are bad conductors of heat; snow does not moisten the living animals buried in it, illustrated by burning camphor in snow

Of the collapse of the sensitive plant

Birds of passage

The acquired habits of plants

Irritability of plants increased by previous exposure to cold

Lichen produces the first vegetation on rocks

Plants holding water

Madder colours the bones of young animals

Colours of animals serve to conceal them

Warm bathing retards old age

Male flowers of Vallisneria detach themselves from the plant, and float to the female ones

Air in the cells of plants, its various uses

How Mr. Day probably lost his life in his diving-ship

Air-bladders of fish

Star-gelly is voided by Herons

Intoxicating mushrooms

Mushrooms grow without light, and approach to animal nature

Seeds of Tillandsia fly on long threads, like spiders on the gossamer

Account of cotton mills

Invention of letters, figures, crotchets

Mrs. Delany's and Mrs. North's paper-gardens

The horologe of Flora

The white petals of Helleborus niger become first red, and then change into a green calyx

Berries of Menispernum intoxicate fish

Effects of opium

Frontispiece by Miss Crewe

Petals of Cistus and Oenanthe continue but a few hours

Method of collecting the gum from Cistus by leathern throngs

Discovery of the Bark

Foxglove how used in Dropsies

Bishop of Marseilles, and Lord Mayor of London

Superstitious uses of plants, the divining rod, animal magnetism

Intoxication of the Pythian Priestess, poison from Laurel-leaves, and from cherry-kernels

Sleep consists in the abolition of voluntary power; nightmare explained

Indian fig emits slender cords from its summit

Cave of Thor in Derbyshire, and sub-terraneous rivers explained

The capsule of the Geranium makes a hygrometer; Barley creeps out of a barn Mr. Edgeworth's creeping hygrometer

Flower of Fraxinella flashes on the approach of a candle

Essential oils narcotic, poisonous, deleterious to insects

Dew-drops from Mancinella blister the skin

Uses of poisonous juices in the vegetable economy

The fragrance of plants a part of their defence

The sting and poison of a nettle

Vapour from Lobelia suffocative; unwholesomness of perfumed hair-powder

Ruins of Palmira

The poison-tree of Java

Tulip roots die annually

Hyacinth and Ranunculus roots

Vegetable contest for air and light

Some voluble stems turn E.S.W. and others W.S.E.

Tops of white Bryony as grateful as asparagus

Fermentation converts sugar into spirit, food into poison

Fable of Prometheus applied to dram-drinkers

Cyclamen buries its seeds and trifolium subterraneum

Pits dug to receive the dead in the plague

Lakes of America consist of fresh water

The seeds of Cassia and some others are carried from America, and thrown on the coasts of Norway and Scotland

Of the gulf-stream

Wonderful change predicted in the gulph of Mexico

In the flowers of Cactus grandiflorus and Cistus some of the stamens are perpetually bent to the pistil

Nyctanthes and others are only fragrant in the night; Cucurbita lagenaria closes when the sun shines on it

Tropeolum, nasturtian, emits sparks in the twilight

Nectary on its calyx

Phosphorescent lights in the evening

Hot embers eaten by bull-frogs

Long filaments of grasses, the cause of bad seed-wheat

Chinese hemp grew in England above 14 feet in five months

Roots of snow-drop and hyacinth insipid like orchis

Orchis will ripen its seeds if the new bulb be cut off

Proliferous flowers

The wax on the candle-berry myrtle said to be made by insects

The warm springs of matlock produced by the condensation of steam raised from great depths by subterranean fires

Air separated from water by the attraction of points to water being less than that of the particles of water to each other

Minute division of sub-aquatic leaves

Water-cress and other aquatic plants inhabit all climates

Butomus esculent; Lotus of Egypt; Nymphæa

Ocymum covered with salt every night

Salt a remote cause of scrophula, and immediate cause of sea-scurvy

Coloured spatha of Arum, and blotched leaves, if they serve the purpose of a coloured petal

Tulip-roots with a red cuticle produce red flowers

Of vegetable mules the internal parts, at those of fructification, resemble the female parent; and the external parts, the male one

The same occurs in animal mules, as the common mule and the hinnus, and in sheep

The wind called Harmattan from volcanic eruptions; some epidemic coughs or influenza have the same origin

Fish killed in the sea by dry summers in Asia

Hedysarum gyrans perpetually moves its leaves like the respiration of animals

Plants possess a voluntary power of motion Loud cracks from ice-mountains explained

Muschus corallinus vegetates below the snow, where the heat is always about 40.

Quick growth of vegetables in northern latitudes after the solution of the snows explained

The Rail sleeps in the snow

Conferva ægagropila rolls about the bottom of lakes

Lycoperdon tuber, truffle, requires no light

Account of caprification

Figs wounded with a straw, and pears and plumbs wounded by insects ripen sooner, and become sweeter

Female figs closed on all sides, supposed to be monsters

Basaltic columns produced by volcanoes shewn by their form

Byssus floats on the sea in the day, and sinks in the night

Conferva polymorpha twice changes its colour and its form

Some seed-vessels and seeds resemble insects

Individuality of flowers not destroyed by the number of males or females which they contain

Trees are swarms of buds, which are individuals

INDEX OF THE NAMES OF THE PLANTS

Adonis
Aegragrópila
Álcea
Amaryllis
Anemóne
Anthoxánthum
Arum
Avéna
Bárometz
Béllis
Byssus
Cáctus
Caléndula
Callítriche
Cánna
Cánnabis
Cápri-fícus
Carlína
Caryophýllus
Cássia
Céreus
Chondrílla
Chunda
Cinchóna
Circæa
Cistus
Cócculus
Cólchicum
Collinsónia
Conférva
Cupréssus
Curcúma
Cuscúta
Cýclamen
Cypérus
Diánthus
Dictámnus
Digitális
Dodecátheon
Drába
Drósera
Dýpsacus
Fícus

Fúcus
Fraxinélla
Galánthus
Genísta
Gloriósa
Gossýpium
Hedýsarum
Heliánthus
Helléborus
Hippómane
Ilex
Impátiens
Iris
Kleinhóvia

Lápsana
Láuro-cérasus
Líchen
Línum
Lobélia
Lonicéra
Lychnis
Lycopérdon
Mancinélla
Méadia
Melíssa
Menispérmum
Mimósa
Múschus
Nymphæa

Ócymum
Orchis
Osmúnda
Osýris
Papáver
Papýrus
Plantágo
Polymórpha
Polypódium
Prúnus
Rúbia

Siléne

Trápa
Tremélla
Tropáeolum
Truffélia
Túlipa
Ulva
Upas
Urtíca
Vallisnéria
Víscum
Vítis
Zostéra

FINIS

CPSIA information can be obtained at www.ICGtesting.com
Printed in the USA
LVOW12s0403110216

474499LV00001B/27/P